ACTIVITY & TEST PREP

ExpressWays

Second Edition

Steven J. Molinsky • Bill Bliss

with

Carolyn Graham

Contributing Author

Dorothy Lynde

Illustrated by

Richard E. Hill

TO THE TEACHER

This enhanced edition of *ExpressWays Activity Workbook 2* includes practice tests designed to prepare students for the types of standardized tests and performance assessments used by many instructional programs to measure and report students' progress. One or two practice tests for each unit of the series simultaneously assess students' achievement of the unit's instructional objectives, provide intensified coverage of lifeskill competencies, and prepare students for standardized general language proficiency tests that assess students' educational advancement and reflect programs' effectiveness in meeting outcome-based performance standards.

The practice tests appear in the second section of this workbook on pages T1–T52. They include: multiple-choice questions that assess vocabulary, grammar, reading, listening skills, lifeskill competencies, and basic literacy tasks (such as reading medicine labels, signs, and everyday documents); writing assessments that can be evaluated using a standardized scoring rubric and collected in portfolios of students' work; and speaking performance assessments designed to stimulate face-to-face interactions between students, for evaluation by the teacher using a standardized scoring rubric, or for self-evaluation by students.

Pages are perforated so that completed tests can be handed in and can serve as a record of students' participation and progress in the instructional program. Scripts for the listening assessment activities are included at the end of this volume and may be removed if desired. An accompanying teacher's volume, the *ExpressWays Activity & Test Prep Workbook 2 Teacher's Resource Book*, includes answer keys, scoring rubrics and guidelines, reproducible learner assessment records for documenting students' progress, teaching suggestions, and test preparation techniques.

ExpressWays, 2nd edition
Activity & Test Prep Workbook 2

Copyright © 2004 by Prentice Hall Regents
Addison Wesley Longman, Inc.
A Pearson Education Company.
All rights reserved.
No part of this publication may be reproduced, stored in a retrieval system, or transmitted in any form or by any means, electronic, mechanical, photocopying, recording, or otherwise, without the prior permission of the publisher.

Pearson Education, 10 Bank Street, White Plains, NY 10606

Editorial director: *Pam Fishman*
Vice president, director of design and production: *Rhea Banker*
Director of electronic production: *Aliza Greenblatt*
Production manager: *Ray Keating*
Director of manufacturing: *Patrice Fraccio*
Associate digital layout manager: *Paula Williams*
Interior design: *Ken Liao*
Cover design: *Warren Fischbach*

The authors gratefully acknowledge the contribution of Tina Carver in the development of the original *ExpressWays* program.

ISBN 0-13-189924-4

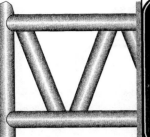

EXPRESSWAYS 2
Activity & Test Prep
Workbook

Exit 1 • Friends and Neighbors

Exit 2 • Calling People Going Places

Exit 3 • Food

Exit 4 • Personal Finances

Exit 5 • At Work

Exit 6 • Rules and Regulations

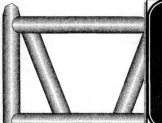

TEST PREPARATION CONTENTS

Exit 1

Greet Someone and Introduce Yourself

Student Text
Pages 2–3

A. Wrong Way!

Put the lines in the correct order.

____ Brazil. And you?

____ Hi. I'm Teresa. Nice to meet you.

____ France.

_1_ Hello. I'm your new neighbor. My name is Louis.

____ Nice meeting you, too. Tell me, where are you from?

B. What's the Response?

Choose the correct response.

1 Where are you from?
   a. My apartment.
   b. Japan.

2 Who did she go with?
   a. To Chicago.
   b. Her neighbor.

3 When did you start your classes?
   a. I started History and English.
   b. I started last week.

4 How are you?
   a. Nice to meet you.
   b. Fine. And you?

5 Who is going to baby-sit?
   a. Jennifer.
   b. Saturday.

6 What does Maria study?
   a. On Monday and Wednesday.
   b. Chinese.

7 Why are you in this class?
   a. I have to learn English.
   b. I have a broken leg.

8 What's your major?
   a. Biology.
   b. Belgium.

9 What floor do you live on?
   a. The 7th.
   b. Apartment 7D.

10 Where are you going?
   a. On Tuesday.
   b. To my apartment.

11 Which apartment do you live in?
   a. 302.
   b. 472-3519.

12 Why can't you go to the movies with us?
   a. I can't go to the movies with you.
   b. I have to do my homework.

1

A. The Right Choice

Circle the correct word.

A. Excuse me. I'm new here. [**Do** / (**Can**)]¹ I ask you a question?

B. Sure.

A. [**Is** / **Are**]² there a park in this [**neighbor** / **neighborhood**]³?

B. Yes. [**There's** / **It's**]⁴ a park around the corner.

A. Around the corner?

B. [**No** / **Yes**]⁵.

A. That's great. Thanks very much.

B. Matching Lines

Match the questions and answers.

_c_	**1** Can I ask you a question?	a. At about 8:30.
___	**2** Where does the superintendent live?	b. Yes, I do.
___	**3** What time does the bus get here?	c. Sure.
___	**4** Is there a laundromat nearby?	d. Yes, I am.
___	**5** Are you happy in your neighborhood?	e. No, they don't.
___	**6** Where's the supermarket?	f. Yes, there is.
___	**7** Does Sally drive to work every day?	g. It's down the block.
___	**8** Do they pick up the garbage today?	h. No. She takes the bus.
___	**9** Do you like your new apartment?	i. He lives in the basement.

Ask Permission to Do Something	Student Text Pages 6–7

A. The Right Choice

Circle the correct word.

A. ((Can) Do)**1** I leave my bicycle here?

B. Yes, you (can   can't)**2**.

A. (Do   Can)**3** I put my garbage here?

B. (No   Yes)**4**, you can't.

B. Listen

Listen and circle the word you hear.

1 can	(can't)	**4** can	can't	**7** can	can't
2 can	can't	**5** can	can't	**8** can	can't
3 can	can't	**6** can	can't	**9** can	can't

C. Sense or Nonsense?

Do the following "make sense" or are they "nonsense"?

		Sense	*Nonsense*
1	"You can go to the laundromat on the corner."	✓	
2	"You can play ball with your friends on the balcony."		
3	"The superintendent lives in the yard."		
4	"You can't leave your bicycle in the hallway."		
5	"You can hang your laundry in the fireplace."		
6	"You can plant flowers in the garden."		
7	"You can park your car in the garbage."		
8	"The bus stop is on the fifth floor."		

Offer to Help Someone

A. Wrong Way!

Put the lines in the correct order.

___ No, not at all.

___ Please. Let me help you.

_1_ Can I help you clean up this mess?

___ Thanks. I appreciate it.

___ Well, all right. If you don't mind.

___ No. That's okay. I can clean it up myself.

B. Listen

Listen and circle the word you hear.

1. (it)   them
2. it   them
3. it   them

4. it   them
5. it   them
6. it   them

7. it   them
8. it   them
9. it   them

C. Fill It In!

Fill in the correct answer.

1. Can I _____ you a question?
   a. ask
   b. use

2. Where can we _____ our laundry?
   a. plant
   b. hang up

3. Please. Let me _____ you.
   a. mind
   b. help

4. Can I _____ here in the yard?
   a. play ball
   b. use my fireplace

5. Excuse me. Where can I _____ my garbage bags?
   a. put
   b. pick up

6. Here. Let me help you _____ these tables.
   a. cut down
   b. put away

7. Thank you very much. I really _____ your help.
   a. thank
   b. appreciate

4

D. Word Search

Find the following words.

| put away | take out | cut down | pick up | hang up | clean up |

```
R I P D G C L O U T S I F Z B B O P
C L E B A C J Y L X W C U T D O W N
D O K E Q Z A C T P R A W L N C M E
T U P I C K U P A N S V P T N P K A
C L O P X E P T A F P U P V P L Z E
L Y W R Y O P G H I S F H K Z C B M
E Q E T U U P A A I P U T A W A Y P
A D G J K R L X N N E T U O S P A G
N K L D R H Y N G L Z W Y O N C P C
U C L T A K E O U T O W P A W A E J
P U T W R C L U P S P W R D E W A P
```

E. Listen

Listen and decide what these people are talking about.

1 (your bags)   your laundry   4 the garbage   the mess

2 the mess   the bags   5 the table   the chairs

3 the laundry   the tree   6 your things   your laundry

F. Wrong Way!

Put the words in the correct order.

1 _____ I can hang it up myself. _____

   it   hang   I   myself.   up   can

2 _____

   ourselves.   We   it   can   up   clean

3 _____

   right   up   Please   them   away.   pick

4 _____

   up   can   He   put   himself.   it

5

Ask a Favor of Someone

A. What's the Line?

Put a check next to the correct line.

B. Matching Lines

Match the lines.

__d__ **1** Alice can't find the bus stop.

____ **2** My friend and I don't have any money.

____ **3** Betty wants to fix a table.

____ **4** Tuesday is their anniversary.

____ **5** Please write me a letter.

____ **6** These shopping bags are heavy.

____ **7** My English homework is difficult.

____ **8** My friends and I love to listen to Mrs. Stoller.

____ **9** Mr. Blaney can't start his car.

____ **10** The Smiths are going to Rio next week.

a. Can you help me with it?

b. Could you help me carry them?

c. We can pick up their mail.

d. Can you help her find it?

e. Let's lend her a hammer.

f. We can help him start it.

g. Let's send them some flowers.

h. Could you lend us some?

i. Let me give you my address.

j. She tells us wonderful stories about her life.

A. The Right Choice

Circle the correct word.

A. You know, I | call / **(called)** |¹ you several times last week, but you | weren't / didn't |² home.

B. No, I | didn't / wasn't |³ . I | did / was |⁴ in San Francisco.

A. Oh. What | were / did |⁵ you do there?

B. I | see / saw |⁶ a wonderful play.

A. Oh. That's nice.

B. Listen

Listen and circle the word you hear.

1	ring	(rang)	9	saw	called
2	have	had	10	were	weren't
3	was	wasn't	11	stopped	stop
4	drive	drove	12	took	look
5	come	came	13	do	did
6	did	didn't	14	went	sent
7	went	want	15	were	weren't
8	heard	read	16	read	saw

7

C. What's the Word?

Complete the sentences.

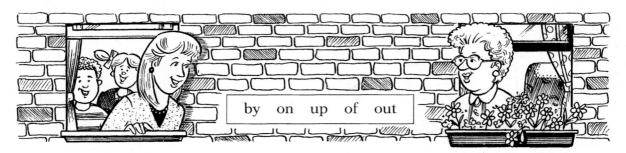

by   on   up   of   out

1 Could you take care _of_ my children this morning?

2 I took ____ the garbage for you.

3 We picked ____ the mail.

4 Please stop ____ my house today.

5 I came ____ yesterday, but you weren't home.

6 I knocked ____ your door.

7 We cleaned ____ the mess.

8 Please help me hang ____ the laundry.

D. What's the Response?

Choose the correct response.

1 Where did you go?
   (a.) I went to work.
   b. I go to work.

2 Why weren't you home?
   a. I wasn't at home.
   b. I was at the supermarket.

3 Who rang the doorbell?
   a. My neighbor rings the doorbell.
   b. My neighbor rang the doorbell.

4 How did you find out about the storm?
   a. I heard it on the radio.
   b. I was on the radio.

5 Did they see a movie yesterday?
   a. Yes. They see a funny comedy.
   b. Yes. They saw a funny comedy.

6 How did you go to the airport?
   a. I drove.
   b. I drive.

7 Did your friend stop by yesterday?
   a. Yes. He stop by at about 6:00.
   b. Yes. He stopped by at about 6:00.

8 Did you clean your apartment today?
   a. Yes, I did.
   b. Yes, I was.

9 Were you at home last week?
   a. No, I didn't. I was in Dallas.
   b. No, I wasn't. I was in Dallas.

10 I went to Los Angeles last week.
   a. Did you visited your cousins?
   b. Did you visit your cousins?

11 What did you do over the weekend?
   a. Nothing special. I was at home.
   b. Nothing special. I did at home.

12 Were you at school this morning?
   a. No, I didn't.
   b. No, I wasn't.

13 Do you want to see the mail?
   a. No, thanks. I saw it already.
   b. No, thanks. I see it already.

14 Was your homework difficult?
   a. No, it weren't.
   b. No, it wasn't.

Give Advice to Someone

Student Text Pages 14–15

A. Wrong Way!

Put the lines in the correct order.

___ I see. And you're trying to fix it yourself?

___ Hmm. You're probably right.

___ I'm trying to fix my stove.

___ What's wrong with it?

_1_ What are you doing?

___ It doesn't work.

___ Yes. But I'm having a lot of trouble.

___ You know, maybe you should call the gas company.

B. Listen

Listen to the conversation and choose the correct answer.

1. (a.) The woman is trying to fix a radiator.
   b. The woman fixed the radiator.
2. a. The radiator is leaking.
   b. The radiator doesn't get hot.
3. a. The woman is having a lot of trouble.
   b. The woman isn't having a lot of trouble.
4. a. Maybe she should call the superintendent.
   b. Maybe she should call a plumber.

C. The 5th Wheel!

Which one doesn't belong?

1	plumber	(sink)	electrician	carpenter
2	toilet	radiator	stove	electrician
3	supermarket	superintendent	apartment	floor
4	around the corner	down the block	in the basement	on Main Street
5	take out	take care of	put away	clean up

D. Crosswalk

electrician	carpenter	plumber	superintendent	gas company

ACROSS

3 The light in the basement doesn't work. We should call the _____.

4 The oven doesn't work. We should call the _____.

5 The heat in the apartment isn't working. We should call the _____.

DOWN

1 My toilet doesn't flush. I should call a _____.

2 Our front door doesn't close. We should call a _____.

3 E L E C T R I C I A N

E. A Good Idea or Not A Good Idea?

Decide if each of these is a good idea or is not a good idea.

		A Good Idea	*Not a Good Idea*
1	"My sink is leaking. I'm going to call a plumber."	✓	
2	"This light doesn't work. I'm going to fix it myself."		
3	"My car doesn't start. I'm going to call Al's Garage."		
4	"My doorbell is broken. I'm going to call the gas company."		
5	"My fireplace doesn't work. I'm going to call the superintendent."		
6	"My stove doesn't go on. I'm going to fix it with a hammer."		
7	"My toilet doesn't flush. I'm going to call an electrician."		
8	"My radiator doesn't get hot. I'm going to put it on the balcony."		

10

A. What's the Line?

Choose the correct lines.

1 ELECTRICIAN: Tally's Wiring Company.

  CUSTOMER: (a.) Hello. Do you fix broken doorbells?
  b. Hello. Are there broken doorbells?

2 ELECTRICIAN: Yes. What's the problem?

  CUSTOMER: a. My doorbell is leaking.
  b. My doorbell doesn't ring.

3 ELECTRICIAN: I see. We can send an electrician at four o'clock this afternoon. Is that okay?

  CUSTOMER: a. Four o'clock this afternoon? Yes, I'm fine.
  b. Four o'clock this afternoon? Yes, that's fine.

4 ELECTRICIAN: Okay. What's the name and the address?

  CUSTOMER: a. The name is Beth Miller, and the address is 57 White Street.
  b. The name is 57 White Street, and the address is Beth Miller.

5 ELECTRICIAN: Phone number?

  CUSTOMER: a. 57 White Street.
  b. 468-2907.

6 ELECTRICIAN: All right. An electrician will be there at four o'clock this afternoon.

  CUSTOMER: a. Thank you.
  b. That's nice.

B. Listen

Listen and decide what these people are talking about.

1 (kitchen sink)   front door   **5** toilet   front door

2 light   toilet   **6** refrigerator   dishwasher

3 refrigerator   radiator   **7** car   stove

4 stove   sink   **8** refrigerator   radiator

C. Analogies

| took | mess | ran | cousins | saw | electrician | sat | weren't |

1 sink : plumber *as* light switch : <u>electrician</u>

2 drive : drove *as* sit : _____

3 grandchild : grandchildren *as* cousin : _____

4 get : got *as* run : _____

5 have : had *as* see : _____

6 was : wasn't *as* were : _____

7 take out : garbage *as* clean up : _____

8 hear: heard *as* take : _____

D. Open Road!

What did you do when something in your home was broken?

When my .... didn't work, I ....

....

E. WordRap: *Home Emergencies*

Listen. Then clap and practice.

A. Quick! Call the plumber!
   Call him today!
B. What should I tell him?
   What should I say?
A. Tell him to hurry!
   Tell him to rush!
   The sink is leaking
   And the toilet doesn't flush!
   Tell him to hurry!
   Tell him to rush!
   The sink is leaking
   And the toilet doesn't flush!

A. Call the electrician!
   Call her today!
B. What should I tell her?
   What should I say?
A. Nothing's working!
   Nothing's right!
   The lights come on
   In the middle of the night!
   Nothing's working!
   Nothing's right!
   The lights come on
   In the middle of the night!

Make Different Kinds of Telephone Calls

A. What's the Word?

Complete the conversation.

Dial	number	area code	"one"	call

A. Excuse me. Could you please tell me how to make a long-distance ____call___ ¹?

B. Sure. _____ ² "one." Dial the _____ ³. Then, dial the local _____ ⁴. Have you got that?

A. I think so. Let me see. I dial _____ ⁵. I dial the _____ ⁶. And then I . . . hmm. Could you repeat the last step?

B. Yes. Dial the local _____ ⁷.

A. Okay. I understand. Thanks very much.

B. Matching Lines

Match the lines.

_d_	❶ Pick up ____.	a. this pay phone
___	❷ Put the money ____.	b. "zero"
___	❸ Give the name of the person ____.	c. in the coin slot
___	❹ Could you tell me how to use ____?	d. the receiver
___	❺ Tell the operator it's a collect ____.	e. number
___	❻ Could you tell me how to make ____?	f. you're calling
___	❼ Dial the area code and the local ____.	g. call
___	❽ Dial ____.	h. a person-to-person call

C. Listen

Listen to the conversation. Check the directions you hear.

<table>
<tr><td>

✔ Dial "zero."

___ Put money in the coin slot.

___ Dial the area code and the local number.

___ Tell the operator it's a collect call.

___ Ask the operator's name.

___ Give your name.

</td><td>

___ Pick up the receiver.

___ Dial "zero."

___ Put the money in the coin slot.

___ Dial the number.

___ Put down the receiver.

___ Tell the operator your name.

</td></tr>
</table>

 1   2

___ Dial "zero."

___ Put the money in the coin slot.

___ Dial the area code and the local phone number.

___ Tell the operator it's a person-to-person call.

___ Give the operator your name.

___ Give the name of the person you're calling.

 3

D. Open Road!

Who do you usually call on the telephone?

Person I call	Local phone call?	Long-distance call?	International call?	Collect call?	Person-to-person call?
My friend Bob	no	yes	yes	no	sometimes

Make Collect and Person-to-Person Calls

A. Wrong Way!

Put the lines in the correct order.

____ What's your name?

____ All right. One moment, please.

_1_ Operator.

____ No. Sally Zeltzer.

____ Sally Zeltzer.

____ I want to make a collect call, please.

____ Did you say "Sally Seltzer"?

B. Listen

Listen and put a check next to the sentence you hear.

1 ____ Is this Larry's Department Store?
   ✔ Is this Lally's Department Store?

2 ____ Do you have any beaches?
   ____ Do you have any peaches?

3 ____ Did you call at seven?
   ____ Did you call at eleven?

4 ____ I fixed the drain.
   ____ I fixed the train.

5 ____ Is the museum open late?
   ____ Is the museum open at eight?

6 ____ I think you're right.
   ____ I think you're light.

7 ____ The collect call was from my father.
   ____ The collect call was from my brother.

8 ____ Do you sell bears?
   ____ Do you sell pears?

9 ____ Is your name Hal?
   ____ Is your name Al?

10 ____ Are you calling Mr. Leardon?
   ____ Are you calling Mr. Reardon?

11 ____ They sell gold watches.
   ____ They sell cold watches.

12 ____ What's the address of the store?
   ____ What's the address on the door?

13 ____ Please come at three.
   ____ Please come and see.

14 ____ Is there a problem with your hearing?
   ____ Is there a problem with your earring?

Leave Telephone Messages

Leave Telephone Messages

Student Text Pages 28–31

A. What's the Response?

Choose the correct response.

1 May I please speak to Mr. Rodriguez?
   a. I'm sorry. He isn't here right now. *(circled)*
   b. Will he be back soon?

2 Mrs. White isn't in. She'll be back in a few hours.
   a. Okay. I'll call back then.
   b. Will she be back soon?

3 When will Emily be back?
   a. I'll call her when she gets back.
   b. She won't be back until 5:00.

4 This is Jim Daniels calling.
   a. Nice meeting you.
   b. Do you want to leave a message?

5 Do you want to leave a message for Louise?
   a. Yes. Please ask her to call me.
   b. I want to talk to Louise.

6 Ben isn't here right now.
   a. Is Ben there?
   b. Oh, I see. When will he be back?

7 Will Mrs. Ferguson be back soon?
   a. She isn't here right now.
   b. She'll be back in a few minutes.

8 Please ask Tom to call me when he gets back.
   a. All right.
   b. Thank you.

9 I'll give them the message.
   a. Okay. I'll call back then.
   b. Thank you.

10 May I ask who's calling?
   a. I'm calling Fred.
   b. This is Anita Lane.

B. WordRap: *Trouble Getting Through!*

Listen. Then clap and practice.

I called Dr. Brown,
But he was out of town.
I called Aunt Lizzie,
But her line was busy.
I called Uncle Fred,
But the line went dead.
I called Irene
And got her answering machine.

I placed a long-distance call
To a friend in Bombay,
And got a machine
That said, "Have a nice day!"

C. Likely or Unlikely?

Is it "likely" or "unlikely" that someone would say the following?

Mr. Drayton will be back in fifteen years.

		Likely	Unlikely
1	"Mr. Drayton will be back in fifteen years."	_____	✓
2	"Please ask Michael to call me when he gets back."	_____	_____
3	"May I please speak to me?"	_____	_____
4	"Mrs. Mazer will be back from lunch in a few days."	_____	_____
5	"This is Bob's dog calling."	_____	_____
6	"I'll give her the message next month."	_____	_____
7	"Please ask her to call me tomorrow."	_____	_____
8	"The electrician will be there after lunch."	_____	_____
9	"The plumber will be there at 2:00 in the morning."	_____	_____
10	"Ramon won't be back from his English class until sometime next year."	_____	_____

D. Matching Lines

Match the questions and answers.

_f_ 1 Will Janet be back soon?

____ 2 Will the bus be on time?

____ 3 Will Mr. and Mrs. Murayama be here soon?

____ 4 Will you call your friend tonight?

____ 5 Will Edward call you collect?

____ 6 Will I get a raise this year?

____ 7 Will it be sunny tomorrow?

____ 8 Will Margaret call her son this morning?

____ 9 Will the mail come soon?

____ 10 Will you and your wife be home tonight?

a. Yes, you will. You'll get a raise in March.

b. Yes, I will. I'll call him after 7:00.

c. Yes, she will. She'll call him at 10:30.

d. No, it won't. It'll be cloudy all day.

e. Yes, we will. We'll be home all evening.

f. No, she won't. She won't be back until 6:00.

g. No, it won't. The bus will definitely be late.

h. No, he won't. He won't call me collect.

i. Yes, it will. The mail will come at noon.

j. Yes, they will. They'll be here at ten.

Purchase Bus, Train, and Airplane Tickets

A. The Right Choice

Circle the correct word.

A. | What [1] | is the next bus to Houston?
(When)

B. It's at | $11.55 [2] |
11:55

A. At | 11:55 [3] |
$11.55

B. Yes.

A. I'd like a round-trip | bus [4] |, please.
ticket

B. All right. That'll be eighteen dollars and fifteen cents | ($18.15) [5] |.
(18:15)

B. Listen

Listen and complete the train schedule.

TRANSAMERICA RAIL SERVICE			
Destination	One-Way Fare	Round-Trip Ticket	Leaves
New York	_____	$64.00	10:10 A.M.
Philadelphia	$43.80	_____	_____
Washington	$52.00	_____	6:48 P.M.
Atlanta	_____	$122.30	11:05 A.M.

18

C. Matching Lines

Match the lines.

_f_	**1**	A noise woke us ＿＿.
＿＿	**2**	We usually eat lunch at ＿＿.
＿＿	**3**	The sun goes down ＿＿.
＿＿	**4**	I usually get home from work at ＿＿.
＿＿	**5**	The sun usually comes up ＿＿.
＿＿	**6**	I usually go to bed at ＿＿.

a. 6:00 in the evening

b. midnight

c. noon

d. at about 5:45 in the morning

e. at around 7:30 in the evening

f. at 2:00 in the morning

D. What's the Response?

Choose the correct response.

1 How much is the ticket?
 a. It's $10.25.
 b. It's 10:25.

2 Where does this bus go?
 a. To Baltimore.
 b. At 9:30.

3 When does the flight to Cairo leave?
 a. It's $114.50.
 b. At 11:45 A.M.

4 What time does Train 57 arrive in Toronto?
 a. It arrives at 12:08.
 b. I arrive at 12:08.

5 Where did you go on vacation?
 a. I go to London.
 b. I went to London.

6 How did you get there?
 a. On Tuesday.
 b. By boat.

7 How much is a one-way ticket to Philadelphia?
 a. It's $275.00.
 b. Which do you prefer?

8 I'd like a round-trip ticket to San Diego.
 a. Is it a round-trip ticket?
 b. Okay. That'll be $87.75.

9 How do you usually travel long-distance?
 a. By collect call.
 b. By plane.

10 When is the next plane to Beijing?
 a. It won't leave soon.
 b. At midnight.

11 How many tickets do you want?
 a. Four tickets, please.
 b. Round-trip, please.

12 Do you prefer the train or the plane?
 a. Yes, I do.
 b. The train.

A. Unscramble and Match

Unscramble the sentences below. Then match them with the appropriate scene.

1

1 _____Please don't lean against the doors!_____

the   don't   Please   doors!   against   lean

2 _____

cars!   between   don't   Please   the   ride

3 _____

belt!   your   seat   fasten   Please

4 _____

don't   bus!   on   radio   Please   your   the   play

5 _____

behind   line!   the   Please   white   stand

6 _____

the   you!   of   your   under   bag   seat   Please   in   put   front

B. What's the Word?

Complete the sentences.

between	under	in front of
behind	on	against

1 The flowers are ____on____ the table.

2 The chair is _____ the fireplace.

3 The purse is _____ the table.

4 The son is leaning _____ the door.

5 The dog is _____ the chair.

6 The daughter is standing _____ her mother and father.

C. Sense or Nonsense?

Do the following "make sense" or are they "nonsense"?

		Sense	*Nonsense*
1	"Please don't stand on that chair!"	✔	
2	"Please stand with the white line!"		
3	"Stand in front of the building!"		
4	"Put your book between the chair!		
5	"Please sit under me!"		
6	"Put the money behind the coin slot!"		
7	"Stand on your son!"		
8	"Please go to the store with your brother!"		
9	"Please don't lean against the door!"		
10	"Please fasten your seat bag!"		
11	"Don't ride your bicycle on the expressway!"		
12	"Please don't go out tonight!"		
13	"Please put away those dishes!"		
14	"Put the cake under the children!"		
15	"Make a collect call!"		
16	"Please don't lean in front of you!"		

Report an Emergency

Student Text Pages 38–41

A. Wrong Way!

Put the lines in the correct order.

____ Did you say Sixth and Seventh Avenue?

____ I want to report an emergency!

____ Where?

____ All right. We'll be there right away.

__1__ Police.

____ What's your name?

____ A man just had a heart attack.

____ Yes. That's right.

____ Michael Chen.

____ On Main Street, between Sixth and Seventh Avenue.

____ Yes. Go ahead.

B. Unscramble the Messages!

Put the following emergency messages in the correct order.

1 _____ _A car just hit a pedestrian._
a   pedestrian.   A   hit   just   car

2 _____
jogger   the   Somebody   mugged   in   a   park.

3 _____
Street.   a   accident   Main   There's   bad   on

4 _____
just   a   store.   Somebody   department   robbed

5 _____
had   heart   A   just   attack.   woman   a

C. What's the Word?

Complete the story.

left	ate	took	woke	saw	sat	went	got

Bill and Melissa _____went_____ [1] to the mall last Saturday to buy a birthday present for their son Tommy. Tommy was going to be three years old on Sunday, and they wanted to buy him a special present. They _____ [2] up early and _____ [3] their apartment at 8:30 A.M. They _____ [4] a bus to the mall. They _____ [5] many wonderful presents for Tommy. There were books, balls, and toy cars. But they really liked the toy trains, and so that's what they _____ [6] him. For lunch, they went to a restaurant in the mall and _____ [7] Italian food. After lunch, they _____ [8] at the table and planned Tommy's birthday party.

D. What's the Question?

Complete the conversation.

How did you get there?	What did you do there?	I'm sorry. What did you say?
Where did you go?	Who did you go with?	What time did the plane leave?

1. _____Where did you go_____ ? I went to Brazil.
2. _____ ? I went by plane.
3. _____ ? I said I went by plane.
4. _____ ? I went with my husband.
5. _____ ? At 2:30 in the afternoon.
6. _____ ? We saw beautiful mountains and beaches.

23

Exit 3

Tell the Quantities of Food You Need to Buy

A. Matching Lines

Match the lines.

_c_ **1** Let's buy a bottle of _____.   a. bananas

____ **2** Let's get a bunch of _____.   b. eggs

____ **3** We need to buy a gallon of _____.   c. ketchup

____ **4** We need a dozen _____.   d. milk

____ **5** Let's get two bags of _____.   e. butter

____ **6** We need a pound of _____.   f. potato chips

____ **7** Let's buy a box of _____.   g. orange juice

____ **8** We need to get a quart of _____.   h. cookies

____ **9** Please get a pint of _____.   i. grapes

____ **10** We need a jar of _____.   j. whole wheat bread

____ **11** Can you get a loaf of _____?   k. ice cream

____ **12** Please buy a bunch of _____.   l. mayonnaise

B. The 5th Wheel!

Which one doesn't belong?

1 milk	lettuce	eggs	butter
2 skim milk	orange juice	rice	apple juice
3 ketchup	apples	oranges	grapes
4 chocolate ice cream	vanilla ice cream	cookies	tuna fish
5 apples	eggs	milk	potato chips
6 quart	half a gallon	half a dozen	gallon
7 jars	quarts	loaves	bottles

C. Crosswalk

ACROSS

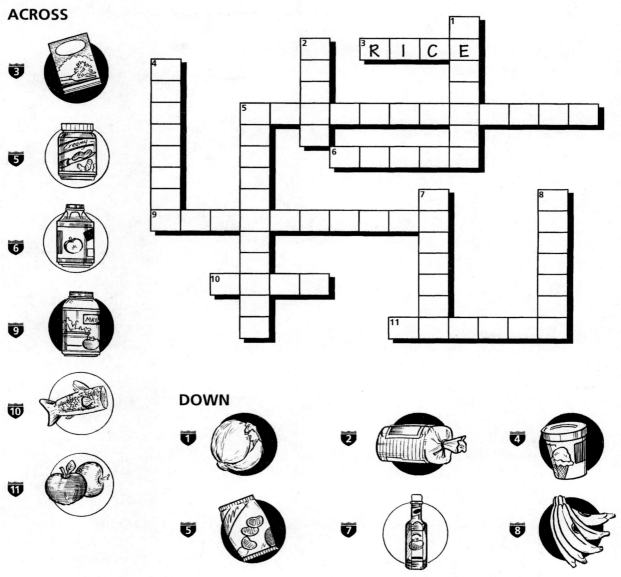

DOWN

D. What's the Word?

Complete the food items.

| head | box | loaf | quart | dozen | can | jar | bag |

1. a _____box_____ of cookies
2. a _____ of bread
3. a _____ of tuna fish
4. a _____ of lettuce

5. a _____ eggs
6. a _____ of orange juice
7. a _____ of potato chips
8. a _____ of mayonnaise

25

A. Wrong Way!

Put the lines in the correct order.

____ All right. That's a dozen hot dogs and two jars of mustard. Is that it?

_1_ May I help you?

____ Anything else?

____ Yes. That's it.

____ Yes. I also want two jars of mustard.

____ Yes, please. I want a dozen hot dogs.

B. Listen

Listen and circle the food item you hear.

1 (a.) a jar of mustard
    b. three jars of mustard

2 a. a pound of roast beef
    b. a pound of ground beef

3 a. a pint of chocolate ice cream
    b. a pound of chocolate ice cream

4 a. two loaf of white bread
    b. two loaves of white bread

5 a. half a pound of Swiss cheese
    b. a pound of Swiss cheese

6 a. a pound of potato salad
    b. one pound of potato salad

7 a. three bottles of mayonnaise
    b. three jars of mayonnaise

8 a. a bag of grapes
    b. a bunch of grapes

9 a. four pounds of chicken
    b. four pieces of chicken

10 a. two dozen rolls
    b. a dozen rolls

C. Matching Lines

Match the lines.

_c_ **1** I want a pound of _____.

____ **2** I'd like a dozen _____.

____ **3** I want six pieces of _____.

____ **4** A loaf of _____, please.

a. rolls

b. white bread

c. ground beef

d. fried chicken

D. Enough or Not Enough?

Are these people going to buy "enough food" or "not enough food" for their guests?

		Enough	Not Enough
1	"My sister is coming over for dinner. I'll need to buy two or three lamb chops."	✓	
2	"I'm going to have a party this weekend. I'll need to buy a hot dog and a loaf of bread."		
3	"My brother is coming over for lunch today. I'll need to buy half a pound of roast beef, some mustard, and two or three rolls."		
4	"My daughter's second-grade class is coming to our house for a party. I'll need to buy two or three donuts and a quart of milk."		

E. WordRap: *May I Help You?*

Listen. Then clap and practice.

A. May I help you?

B. Yes, please.
   I'd like a dozen hot dogs,
   A can of peas,
   A jar of mustard,
   And a pound of cheese,
   Two pounds of beef,
   And a box of rice.
   We're having a picnic.

A. Oh, that's nice!

A. Anything else?

B. Let me see.
   I'd like two large jars
   Of strawberry jam,
   A loaf of bread,
   And a pound of ham,
   Two heads of lettuce
   And some onions, too.
   Do you deliver?

A. Of course, we do!

F. Open Road!

You're going to have a picnic with some friends this weekend. Make a shopping list.

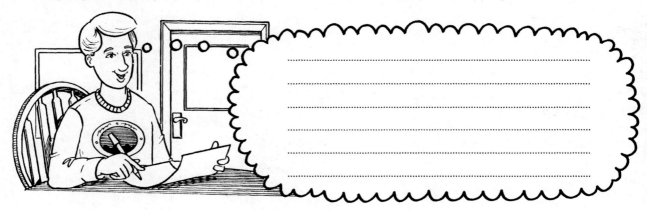

Pay for Food Items and Receive Change

A. Wrong Way!

Put the lines in the correct order.

____ All right. Your change is sixteen dollars and forty-two cents.

____ Yes.

____ Thank you.

_1_ That'll be three fifty-eight.

____ Have a nice day.

____ Here's twenty.

____ Three fifty-eight?

B. Matching Lines

Match the lines.

_e_ **1** forty-eight cents

____ **2** thirty dollars and twenty-six cents

____ **3** one ninety-nine

____ **4** eight dollars and five cents

____ **5** thirteen dollars and twenty-six cents

a. $13.26

b. $1.99

c. $30.26

d. $8.05

e. $·.48

C. What's the Change?

What change will you receive?

1 A. That'll be $6.47 with tax.
   B. Here's ten.
   A. Your change is _____

   _____.

2 A. That comes to $56.98.
   B. Here's a hundred.
   A. Okay. Your change is _____

   _____.

D. Listen

Listen and decide if the prices are "likely" or "unlikely."

1 likely (unlikely) **3** likely unlikely **5** likely unlikely

2 likely unlikely **4** likely unlikely **6** likely unlikely

28

Order Food in a Fast-Food Restaurant

A. The Right Choice

Circle the correct word.

A. Welcome to Carolina Fried Chicken. May I help you?

B. I'd like two cups / (pieces) ¹ of chicken and an container / order ² of french fries.

A. Do you want anything to drink with that?

B. Yes. I'll have a cup / order ³ of coffee.

A. Okay. Is that for here or to eat / go ⁴ ?

B. For here / her ⁵ .

A. That comes to four dollars and twenty-three cents, please.

B. Here you are.

A. And here's your order / change ⁶ . Your food will be ready in a moment.

B. Listen

Listen and circle the correct answer.

1. (fries)   shake
2. tacos   coffee
3. small salad   hamburgers

4. sandwich   soda
5. iced tea   chicken
6. cheeseburger   cole slaw

29

C. Listen

Listen to the order and choose the correct item.

1 ___ two large orders of french fries

✔ a large order of french fries

2 ___ a cup of cole slaw

___ a cup of coffee

3 ___ twelve tacos

___ two tacos

4 ___ three pieces of chicken

___ three large chickens

5 ___ an order of french fries

___ an order of refried beans

6 ___ a chocolate shake

___ a chocolate soda

7 ___ a ground beef sandwich

___ a roast beef sandwich

8 ___ two fish salads

___ two fish sandwiches

9 ___ a medium Coke

___ a small Coke

10 ___ three cheeseburgers

___ three hamburgers

D. Mix-Up!

The orders are all mixed up! Put the words in the correct order.

> *I'd like a cup of fries and an order of coffee.*

___I'd like an order of fries and___

___a cup of coffee.___

1

> *Ten pieces of soda and a small orange chicken, please.*

_____

_____

2

> *I'll have a roast beef iced tea and a medium sandwich.*

_____

_____

3

> *I'd like a vanilla sandwich and a fish shake.*

_____

_____

4

> *I'd like a container of lemonade and a medium cole slaw.*

_____

_____

5

Order Food in a "Sit-Down" Restaurant

Student Text
Pages 54–55

A. What's the Response?

Choose the correct response.

1. What would you like?
   a. I like fish.
   b. I'd like the fish. ⟵ (circled)

2. Would you prefer noodles or rice?
   a. I'd prefer noodles.
   b. I prefer noodles.

3. Would you like anything to drink?
   a. Yes. I'd like a glass of mineral water.
   b. No. I'd like a glass of mineral water.

B. Wrong Way!

Put the lines in the correct order.

___ Two more glasses? Of course.

___ Yes. Could we please have two more glasses of iced tea?

___ Could you also take back this potato? It isn't cooked.

_1_ Is everything all right with your meal?

___ Well, actually this roast beef is cold.

___ I see. Anything else?

___ I'm terribly sorry. I'll take it back to the kitchen.

C. Food Match

Match the words and the food items.

noodles	meat loaf	rice	spaghetti
mashed potatoes	baked beans	fish	lamb chops

1. _fish_

2. _____

3. _____

4. _____

5. _____

6. _____

7. _____

8. _____

31

D. Listen

Listen and circle the correct answer.

1	coffee	(milk)		4	rice	tea
2	potatoes	fries		5	beans	potato
3	loaf	chops		6	Pepsi	noodles

E. Scrambled Foods

Unscramble the following foods.

1	t t a o o p	_____potato_____		4	k i e c c n h	_____
2	s o n d e l o	_____		5	m b a l s o h c p	_____
3	h i a e t s t g p	_____		6	d e b k a a n s e b	_____

F. The 5th Wheel!

Which one doesn't belong?

1	coffee	(beans)	tea	water
2	iced	rice	noodles	beans
3	lamb chops	fish	chicken	roast beef
4	want	help	like	prefer

G. Open Road!

You're ordering dinner at a restaurant. Order anything you'd like.

A. May I help you?

B. Yes. I'll have ....

A. And what would you like with that?

B. Let me see. I'd like ....

A. And would you like anything to drink?

B. Hmm. I think I'll have ....

A. Okay. That's ....

    with .... and a

    ....

Be a Guest at Someone's Dinner Table

A. The Right Choice

Circle the correct word.

A. Would you like a [little / (few)]¹ more mushrooms?

B. [It's / They're]² excellent . . . but no, thank you.

A. Oh, come on! Have a [few / little]³ more.

B. All right. But please . . . not too [much / many]⁴ .

A. Would you like a [little / few]⁵ more pie?

B. [They're / It's]⁶ very good . . . but no, thank you.

A. Oh, come on! Have a [few / little]⁷ more.

B. All right. But please . . . not too [much / many]⁸ .

B. Listen

Listen and circle the correct answer.

1. meatballs   (ice cream)   3. meat loaf   baked potatoes
2. cookies   salad   4. noodles   rice

C. What's the Word?

Complete the following.

few   little   many   much

Bob likes to go to his friend Sally's house for dinner. Sally is a very good cook. How _____much_____ [1] food does Bob eat at Sally's house? He always eats too _____ [2]! Sally makes a very good salad. Bob tries to eat only a _____ [3], but he usually eats too _____ [4]. Sally also makes fantastic meatballs! Bob always eats too _____ [5]. When Sally offers him more meatballs, he always eats a _____ [6] more. For dessert, there are usually cookies and ice cream. Bob thinks that Sally's cookies are wonderful! How _____ [7] cookies does he eat? Too _____ [8]! And how _____ [9] ice cream does he eat? You guessed it! He always eats too _____ [10]!

D. Matching Lines

Match the lines.

_c_ **1** How _____ tacos do you want?   a. much

_____ **2** How _____ salad is left?   b. little

_____ **3** May I have a _____ more egg rolls?   c. many

_____ **4** I'd like a _____ more bread and cheese.   d. few

E. Open Road!

Roger made a New Year's resolution this year. He says he isn't going to eat too many cookies or too much ice cream! How about you? Do you have any resolutions?

Next year ....

....

....

A. The Right Choice

Circle the correct word.

A. Your stew is delicious. Can you tell me the recipe?

B. Sure. First, (add (mix))¹ together meatballs, onions, mushrooms, and carrots.

A. I see.

B. Then, (add   put)² salt and (add   put)³ the mixture in a pan. Are you with me so far?

A. Yes. I'm following you.

B. Okay. Next, (bake   serve)⁴ it in the oven for one and a half hours at 375 degrees.

A. Uh-húh.

B. And then, (bake   serve)⁵ it with bread and a salad. Have you got all that?

A. Yes, I've got it. Thanks.

B. Listen

Listen and put the recipe instructions in the correct order.

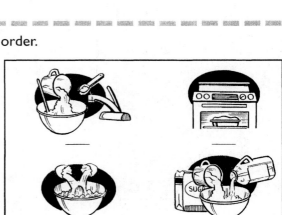

C. Matching Lines

Match the lines.

_c_ **1** Can you tell me the recipe?

____ **2** Tell me, are the chocolate chip cookies easy to make?

____ **3** Do you like to eat at McDon's fast food restaurant?

____ **4** How many do you want?

____ **5** How much cake do you want?

____ **6** Are supermarkets convenient?

____ **7** Did you say seventeen dollars? Here's twenty.

____ **8** Is that for here or to go?

a. I'd like just a little, please.

b. Yes. I love the hamburgers and the french fries there.

c. Sure. First, mix together some butter and sugar.

d. And your change is three dollars.

e. Not too many. Just a few.

f. It's for here.

g. Yes. You can shop for food in just one place and save time.

h. Yes, they are. The recipe is very easy.

D. What's the Word?

Complete the food items.

| water | slaw | loaf | chicken | fries | dogs |
| chops | beans | tea | beef | chips | cream |

1 fried _chicken_

2 lamb _____

3 roast _____

4 meat _____

5 french _____

6 refried _____

7 mineral _____

8 iced _____

9 cole _____

10 hot _____

11 potato _____

12 ice _____

E. Open Road!

Give instructions for your favorite recipe.

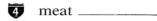

My recipe for ....

First, ...

Then, ...

Next, ...

And then, ...

A. The Right Choice

Circle the correct word.

1. When / (Where) are you from?

2. Why / Which are you here?

3. When / Who did you call them?

4. Which / Who floor do you live on?

5. When / What are you doing?

6. Who / What do you call collect?

7. Why / When is the next train to Chicago?

8. What / Who do you order at that restaurant?

B. What's the Word?

Complete the sentences.

me	him	her	us	you	them

1. Here's my address. Please write __*me*__ a letter.

2. It's my sister's birthday tomorrow. I'm going to send _____ flowers.

3. My new neighbors are very nice. I want you to meet _____.

4. We're going to plant a garden. Do you want to help _____?

5. Richard can't find his wallet. Can you lend _____ some money?

6. I'll be glad to help _____ do your English homework.

7. I'm making chocolate chip cookies. Can you give _____ a few eggs?

C. The Right Choice

Circle the correct word.

1 Put (off / **away**) the dishes.

2 Take (up / out) the garbage.

3 Pick (away / up) the mess.

4 Get (up / off) the train.

5 Cut (down / out) those trees.

6 Put (off / away) the books.

7 Mix (together / from) the ingredients.

8 Clean (up / down) the kitchen.

D. Listen

Listen and circle the word you hear.

1 buy (**bought**)   **4** sat sit   **7** get got

2 spent spend   **5** ride rode   **8** wake up woke up

3 take took   **6** had have   **9** eat ate

E. The Right Choice

Circle the correct word.

1 ((**Is**) Does) there a bus stop nearby?

2 We need a (pound quart) of milk.

3 I (wasn't didn't) hear you.

4 (Am Can) I leave my bike here?

5 I'd like a (bunch head) of bananas.

6 How (much many) eggs do we have?

7 He (won't don't) be here until Friday.

8 (Was Did) you hear something?

9 The stove (isn't doesn't) working.

10 (Do Will) he be back soon?

11 Have a (little few) more salad.

12 (Do May) I speak to Mr. Jansen?

13 (Could Would) I please have a cup of tea?

14 What are you (do doing)?

Exit 4

Evaluate the Affordability of Items in a Store

Student Text
Pages 66–69

A. The Right Choice

Circle the correct answer.

A. Which chair do you like?

B. I like this one. It's very ((nice) nicer)[1].

A. I know. It's (nice   nicer)[2] than that one, but it's also (expensive   more expensive)[3].

B. Hmm. You're right.

A. I don't think we can afford it.

B. I suppose not.

B. More Right Choices

Circle the correct answer.

1. This small fan is more powerful than that large one. Let's buy the ((small) large) one.

2. The blue chair is more comfortable than the yellow one. I think we should buy the (blue   yellow) one.

3. Let's buy this air conditioner. It's (noisier   quieter) than that one.

4. I like this rug very much. It's much (uglier   prettier) than that one.

5. I think that crib is much (more powerful   nicer) than this one.

6. This dishwasher is (more expensive   cheaper) than that one. I don't think we can afford it.

7. I like this CD player. It's much (more comfortable   better) than that one.

8. These brown shoes are much more attractive than those black shoes over there. I think you should buy the (brown   black) shoes.

9. Of course we can afford this computer. It's (more expensive   cheaper) than the computer at the other store.

10. This shirt is too large. You need to buy a (larger   smaller) one.

11. Mommy, I like this doll better than that doll. It's (prettier   uglier) than that one. And you'll be happy because it's also (more expensive   cheaper).

39

C. Matching Lines

Match the lines.

_a_ **1** This washing machine isn't very quiet.

___ **2** This sofa is nicer than that one.

___ **3** These gloves are more comfortable than those gloves.

___ **4** Those shirts are cheaper than these shirts.

___ **5** This rug isn't very attractive.

___ **6** This CD player is better than that one.

a. You're right. Let's buy that one.

b. I agree. Let's buy this one.

c. That's true. I think we should buy those.

d. I agree. I think we should buy these.

e. I agree. We should buy it.

f. I know. We shouldn't buy it.

D. Crosswalk

S M A L L E R

ACROSS

2 Those gloves are very large. Try these gloves. They're _____ than those.

5 A color TV is more expensive than a black-and-white TV. A black-and-white TV is _____.

6 That doll is ugly! We need to find a _____ one.

7 This air conditioner is very noisy! I need to buy a _____ one.

DOWN

1 This rug isn't very attractive. That one is _____.

3 That computer isn't very powerful. I think this one is _____.

4 This crib isn't very good. I need to buy a _____ one.

Evaluate the Affordability of Items in a Store

Student Text Pages 70–73

A. Wrong Way!

Put the lines in the correct order.

—— Take a look at this one. It's the most dependable dryer in the store.

—— Three hundred and seventy-five dollars.

_1_ May I help you?

—— Of course. I'll be happy to.

—— I see. Can you show me a less expensive one?

—— Yes. I'm looking for a dependable dryer.

—— How much is it?

B. Description Match

Write the correct description under each picture.

the firmest	the most talkative	the most comfortable
the most nutritious	the most dangerous	the most powerful
the most expensive	the quietest	the most lightweight

1 _the most lightweight_

2 _____

3 _____

4 _____

5 _____

6 _____

7 _____

8 _____

9 _____

41

C. Listen

Listen to the advertisements and check the words you hear.

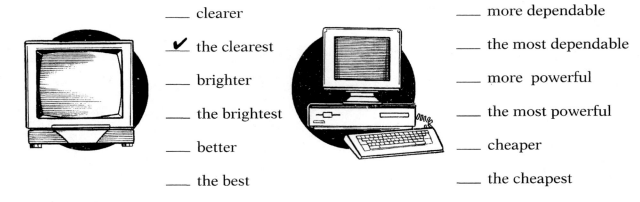

___ clearer

✔ the clearest

___ brighter

___ the brightest

___ better

___ the best

___ more dependable

___ the most dependable

___ more powerful

___ the most powerful

___ cheaper

___ the cheapest

1 *the Magnabox TV*

2 *the McDougal computer*

D. The Right Choice

Circle the correct answer.

1 This is the (firmer (firmest)) mattress in the store.

2 I like this bookcase. It's (larger   largest) than that one over there.

3 I'm looking for a (best   good) cassette player.

4 Is this the (big   biggest) table you have?

5 This is very expensive. Can you show me a (cheaper   more expensive) one?

6 I'm looking for the (more lightweight   most lightweight) sweater you have.

7 Can you please show me a less (expensive   cheaper) one?

8 These gloves are (the most comfortable   more comfortable) than those.

E. Sense or Nonsense?

Do the following "make sense" or are they "nonsense"?

		Sense	*Nonsense*
1	"Don't buy these shoes. They're comfortable."	_____	✔
2	"This is a powerful computer. We should buy it."	_____	_____
3	"Let's buy this sofa. It isn't very attractive."	_____	_____
4	"Let's buy this stereo. It's the best one they have."	_____	_____
5	"I don't like talkative parrots. Let's buy this one. It's very quiet."	_____	_____
6	"I think we should buy this dryer. It's less dependable than that one."	_____	_____

42

Budget Your Money

Student Text
Pages 74–75

A. The Right Choice

Circle the correct word. Then decide on the amount of money.

A. You know . . . I think we ((should) had to)[1] stop at the bank.

B. Why? Do we need cash?

A. Yes. Remember . . . We (have to   has to)[2] get
an anniversary gift for your parents, and we're
(have to   going)[3] to visit your brother on Saturday.

B. You're right. I forgot. How much do you think we
(has to   should)[4] get?

A. I think .... will be enough.

B. I think so, too.

B. Matching Lines

Match the lines.

<u>d</u> **1** We're going skiing tomorrow.

____ **2** Rita doesn't have any gas in her car.

____ **3** We should stop at the bank.

____ **4** How much do you think we should get?

____ **5** I have a big English exam this Friday.

a. You're right. We need cash.

b. Do you have to study all week?

c. She has to buy some.

d. Do you have to rent skis?

e. Fifty dollars will be enough.

C. WordRap: *Money Problems!*

Listen. Then clap and practice.

A. Maybe we should get some money, honey.
   Maybe we should cash a check.

B. Maybe we should go to the bank, Frank.
   Our weekly budget is a wreck!

A. Our weekly budget is a wreck?!

B. Yes! Our weekly budget is a wreck!

A. I need some change for the phone, Joan.
   We need some money for the rent.

B. But we can't get cash from the cash machine.
   'Cause all of our money is spent!

A. All of our money is spent?!

B. Yes! All of our money is spent!

43

A. What's the Response?

Choose the correct response.

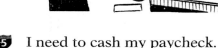

1 I'd like to deposit this in my savings account.
  - (a.) Please print your name on the deposit slip.
  - b. Please cash this check.

2 I'd like to cash this check.
  - a. Yes, you do.
  - b. Please write your account number on the back.

3 Did I forget to sign the check?
  - a. Yes, you did.
  - b. Yes, you do.

4 I'd like to make a withdrawal.
  - a. Please sign your name on the deposit slip.
  - b. Please sign your name on the withdrawal slip.

5 I need to cash my paycheck.
  - a. Please endorse it.
  - b. Please sign the withdrawal slip.

6 I'd like to deposit this in my account.
  - a. Put your address on the deposit slip, please.
  - b. Put your money on the deposit slip, please.

B. Open Road!

Follow the instructions.

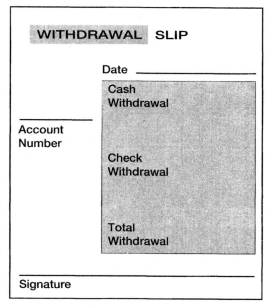

WITHDRAWAL SLIP

Date _____

Cash Withdrawal

Account Number

Check Withdrawal

Total Withdrawal

Signature

Withdraw money from your account. Make a cash withdrawal and a check withdrawal.

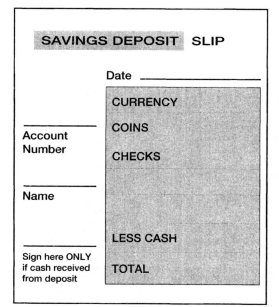

SAVINGS DEPOSIT SLIP

Date _____

CURRENCY

Account Number

COINS

CHECKS

Name

Sign here ONLY if cash received from deposit

LESS CASH

TOTAL

Deposit a check in your account. Get some cash back.

Discuss Balancing a Checkbook

Student Text
Pages 78–79

A. Wrong Way!

Put the lines in the correct order.

____ Oh. I forgot to tell you. I wrote a check to Barry's Clothing for a skirt and a sweater.

____ Okay. Thanks.

__1__ What are you doing?

____ Yes. Sixty-six dollars.

____ I'm balancing the checkbook.

____ Oh. Do you remember the amount?

B. Listen

Listen and circle the word you hear.

1	(textbooks)	tests	6	CDs	TVs
2	textbook	checkbook	7	credit card bill	checking account bill
3	$25.00	$125.00	8	$152.60	$162.50
4	amount	account	9	vitamins	medicine
5	$30.00	$13.00	10	sign	endorse

C. Open Road!

You just bought something special. Now you have to pay for it. Write a check.

PAY TO THE
ORDER OF _____ $ _____

_____ Dollars

FOR _____

2:364967:0055

45

A. Coin Match

Match the coin with its name.

| penny — 1 cent | nickel — 5 cents | dime — 10 cents | quarter — 25 cents |

1 _____ quarter _____

_____ 25 cents _____

2 _____

_____

3 _____

_____

4 _____

_____

B. What's the Word?

| penny — pennies | nickel — nickels | dime — dimes | quarter — quarters |

1 A. I'm going to get some soda. Do you want anything?

B. Sure. Please get me a soda, too. That's sixty-five cents, right?

A. Yes, sixty-five cents.

B. Okay. Here's two quarters, a dime, and a _____ nickel _____ .

2 A. I'm going to get some ice cream. Do you want anything?

B. Sure. Please get me a cup of vanilla ice cream. That's eighty cents, right?

A. Yes, eighty cents.

B. Okay. Here's a nickel and three _____ .

3 A. I'm trying to buy a cup of coffee, but I just lost my money!

B. What did you put in?

A. A quarter, two nickels, and a _____ .

B. Forty-five cents? That's too bad!

4 A. I'm trying to buy some gum, but I just lost my money!

B. What did you put in?

A. Nine _____ .

B. Nine cents! That's too bad!

A. What's the Date?

Complete each sentence with the correct date.

1. Tom and Jane Ross have to pay the telephone bill on __September second__.

2. The cable TV bill isn't due yet. It's due on _____.

3. They have to pay the gas bill soon. It's due on _____.

4. Jane is sure the water bill is due on _____.

5. They have to pay the oil bill on _____.

6. The electric bill is due on _____.

B. Matching Lines

Match the months with their abbreviations.

_f_ **1** June   a. APR

____ **2** December   b. JUL

____ **3** May   c. AUG

____ **4** February   d. OCT

____ **5** August   e. MAR

____ **6** January   f. JUN

____ **7** November   g. SEPT

____ **8** March   h. FEB

____ **9** September   i. DEC

____ **10** April   j. NOV

____ **11** October   k. JAN

____ **12** July   l. MAY

47

C. Listen

Marcia is very busy this month. There are a lot of dates in June she has to remember. Listen and write the number of each special occasion on Marcia's calendar.

JUNE						
Sunday	**Monday**	**Tuesday**	**Wednesday**	**Thursday**	**Friday**	**Saturday**
___ 1	___ 2	___ 3	___ 4	_1_ 5	___ 6	___ 7
___ 8	___ 9	___ 10	___ 11	___ 12	___ 13	___ 14
15	16	17	18	19	20	21
___ 22	___ 23	___ 24	___ 25	___ 26	___ 27	___ 28
___ 29	___ 30					

D. Wrong Way!

Unscramble the words.

1. h f i f t   _____fifth_____
2. o s d n e c   _____
3. h r i t t i t e h   _____
4. w n i t t e t h e   _____
5. r o h f u t   _____
6. t d i h r   _____

E. Open Road!

Complete the following.

1. What's your favorite day of the year? ....

   Why? ....

2. In your opinion, what's the most exciting day of the year? ....

   Why? ....

A. Wrong Way!

Put the lines in the correct order.

____ All right, Ms. Rodriguez. Please hold, and I'll check our records.

____ I believe I was charged too much.

____ Finally, what is the amount on your bill?

____ Thank you.

_1_ Vision Cable Company. May I help you?

____ And what is your account number, Ms. Rodriguez?

____ Seventy-six dollars and fifteen cents ($76.15).

____ Oh. What's the problem?

____ Carmen Rodriguez.

____ 677-4533-9812-003.

____ I see. I need some information. First, what is your name?

____ Yes. I think there's a mistake on my cable TV bill.

B. The 5th Wheel!

Which one doesn't belong?

1	(dollar bill)	penny	nickel	quarter
2	car payment	electric bill	paycheck	mortgage payment
3	checkbook	kitchen table	account number	check register
4	budget	expenses	savings	apples
5	oil bill	make a deposit	make a withdrawal	cash a check
6	crib	cassette player	computer	stereo system
7	JAN	SAT	OCT	JUL
8	first	three	fourth	fifth
9	nicer	better	best	more powerful

C. Listen

Listen to the conversations and choose the correct answer.

1. (a.) The amount isn't correct.
    b. The account isn't correct.

2. a. The gas bill is for $30.00.
    b. The gas bill is for $300.00.

3. a. This person checked the account balance with a calculator.
    b. This person balanced the calculator.

4. a. This person writes down what she spends each month.
    b. This person doesn't write down her monthly expenses.

5. a. This person adds a lot to his savings account every month.
    b. This person knows how much he can add to his savings account every month.

6. a. This person's telephone bill is due on the 20th.
    b. This person will get a telephone on the 20th.

7. a. This person has to cash a check.
    b. This person has to write a check.

8. a. There's a mistake on the tuition bill.
    b. This person asks the amount of a tuition bill.

D. A Good Idea or Not a Good Idea?

Decide if each of these is a good idea or is not a good idea.

		A Good Idea	Not a Good Idea
1	"Balance your checkbook every month!"	✓	
2	"Buy a car you can't afford!"		
3	"Buy products on sale!"		
4	"Stop at a bank to get cash!"		
5	"Buy gloves that aren't comfortable!"		
6	"Spend all your money every week!"		
7	"Save some money every month!"		
8	"Enter information about every check in your check register!"		
9	"First, decide on a product you want to buy. Second, compare prices at two different stores. Third, buy the product at the most expensive price."		

Make Requests

Student Text Pages 88–89

A. What's the Word?

Complete the conversations.

her	him	them

1 Please fax this report to the company directors.

Certainly. I'll ___fax them___ the report this afternoon.

2 Will you give this package to Mr. Lee on the first floor?

Sure. I'll _____ the package right away.

3 Please mail this letter to my daughter.

Certainly. I'll _____ the letter right now.

4 Can you read a story to the children?

Of course. I'll _____ a story right now.

5 Please send an e-mail to the customers.

Certainly. I'll _____ an e-mail right away.

6 Will you please write a thank-you note to your grandmother?

Okay. I'll _____ a thank-you note this afternoon.

B. Matching Lines

Which of these go together?

_d_ **1** fax machine

___ **2** computer

___ **3** telephone

___ **4** Shipping Department

___ **5** announcement

a. numbers

b. news

c. e-mail

d. fax a memo

e. packages

Offer to Help Somebody at Work

Student Text Pages 90–91

A. What's the Line?

Complete the conversations.

1
Do you want me to clean up the office?

No. That's okay. I can ___clean it up___ later.

2
Would you like me to set up the conference room?

Yes. Please _____ right now.

3
Would you like me to hang up these signs?

Thanks. Can you _____ _____ today?

4
Do you want me to give out these memos?

Good idea! Please _____ now.

5
Do you want me to put away the dishes?

No, that's okay. I can _____ _____ later.

6
I'll be happy to take down the decorations.

Thanks. Please _____ _____ anytime.

B. Listen

Listen and circle the correct answer.

1 (take them down)   take him down   **4** clean it up   clean them up

2 call them   call him   **5** give him   give them

3 put them away   put him away   **6** hang them up   hang up

52

C. The 5th Wheel!

Which one doesn't belong?

1	memo	note	letter	(telephone)
2	package	computer	fax machine	telephone
3	factory	office	mechanic's garage	computer
4	give out	up	put away	clean up
5	over there	right now	anytime today	right away
6	conference room	supply room	mail room	reports
7	customer	announcement	Mr. Jones	Ms. Sanchez

D. Open Road!

Write your own sentences.

take down	set up	put away	hang up	give out	clean up

1 ....

....

2 ....

....

3 ....

....

4 ....

....

5 ....

....

6 ....

....

53

Give Feedback at Work

Student Text Pages 92–93

A. The Right Choice

Circle the correct word.

1 You paint very (careful (carefully))!

2 You're a very (fast   faster) assembler!

3 You're a very (neatly   neat) worker!

4 Mrs. Wong teaches very (well   good)!

5 You dance very (gracefully   graceful)!

6 You're a very (accurately   accurate) worker!

B. Analogies

teaches	acts	accurate	positive feedback
well	waiter	dancer	computer

1 dancer : dances *as* teacher : _____ *teaches*

2 translator : translates *as* actor : _____

3 accurate : translator *as* graceful : _____

4 carefully : careful *as* accurately : _____

5 neat : neatly *as* good : _____

6 fax : fax machine *as* e-mail : _____

7 assemble : assembler *as* waits on tables : _____

8 "That's bad!" : negative feedback *as* "That's good!" : _____

C. Listen

Who am I? Listen and circle the correct answer.

1 (dancer)   typist

2 assembler   teacher

3 translator   actor

4 waiter   typist

5 assembler   dancer

6 teacher   painter

7 translator   waiter

8 teacher   mechanic

9 actor   assembler

10 translator   interviewer

11 student   teacher

12 typist   police officer

D. Open Road!

How do you do the following things?

| accurately | gracefully | neatly | carefully | well | fast |

I sing very well.

I don't dance very gracefully.

I work very neatly.

1 I sing ....

2 I dance ....

3 I act ....

4 I work ....

5 I translate ....

6 I speak English ....

7 I paint ....

8 I type ....

9 I assemble things ....

10 I cook ....

11 I balance my checkbook ....

12 I ....

13 I ....

14 I ....

E. WordRap: *Good Workers*

Listen. Then clap and practice.

He's a very good typist.
He types very well.
He types very quickly.
And he knows how to spell.

She's a wonderful dancer.
She dances very well.
She dances very gracefully.
Can't you tell?

We're very fast assemblers.
We're extremely quick.
Our work is always finished,
Even when we're sick.

They're very good painters.
They have what it takes.
They paint very carefully.
They never make mistakes.

Ask for and Give Feedback

A. What's the Response?

Choose the correct response.

1 Am I working fast enough?
    (a.) Yes, you are.
    b. No. You should try to work more politely.

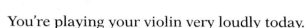

2 You're playing your violin very loudly today.
    a. I'll try to play it louder.
    b. I'll try to play it softer.

3 Am I dancing gracefully enough?
    a. You should try to dance more gracefully.
    b. You should try to dance more neatly.

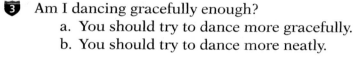

4 Am I explaining this well enough?
    a. Yes. You're explaining it very well.
    b. Yes. You should explain it better.

5 You should try to speak to your teachers more politely.
    a. Should I speak more politely?
    b. Okay. I'll try to speak more politely.

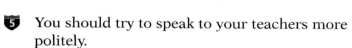

6 You aren't doing this carefully enough.
    a. Thank you.
    b. I'll try to work more carefully.

7 You really should work more quickly.
    a. Okay. I'll try to work a little faster.
    b. Thank you. I'll try to work more slowly.

B. Crosswalk

ACROSS

2. You don't drive very carefully. You should try to drive ________.
4. You're typing too slowly. You should type ________.
6. Some waiters don't speak politely. They should try to speak ________.

DOWN

1. You didn't paint very well last week. Please try to paint ________.
3. You don't usually speak loudly enough. Please try to speak ________.
5. You don't drive your car very slowly. Please try to drive ________.

C. The Right Choice

Circle the correct word.

1. Roland, you aren't playing your guitar loud enough. You ((should) shouldn't) try to play it louder.
2. Arthur (is isn't) a good cashier. He doesn't speak very politely to the customers.
3. Mrs. Anderson (speaks doesn't speak) very slowly. I understand everything she says.
4. Carmen (is isn't) very accurate. She's a very good employee.
5. Richard (is isn't) a very good dancer. He should try to dance more gracefully.
6. Michael (works doesn't work) very slowly. He should try to work faster.
7. Alice (is isn't) a very careful painter. She should try to paint more carefully.
8. You're a very good typist. You (type don't type) very well.
9. Patty is a fast assembler. She works very (quickly slowly).
10. Mrs. Chen is a very accurate translator. She (always never) makes mistakes.
11. Mr. Greenley (is isn't) a very good teacher. He doesn't explain things very well.

Apologize

**Student Text
Pages 96–99**

A. The Right Choice

Circle the correct answer.

1 A. I'm sorry. (I'll be able to (I won't be able to)) attend your press conference this afternoon.
B. Oh? Why not?
A. I (have to   had to) welcome a visitor from Brazil.
B. No problem. It's okay.

2 A. I'm sorry that I (was able to   wasn't able to) work late last Friday.
B. That's all right.
A. The reason is that I (have to   had to) go to the dentist.
B. I understand. Don't worry about it.

3 A. I'm sorry that I (could   couldn't) finish the report yesterday.
B. That's all right.
A. The reason is that I (have to   had to) meet with my supervisor.
B. I understand. Don't worry about it.

B. Listen

Yesterday or tomorrow? Listen and circle the correct answer.

1	(yesterday)	tomorrow	**8**	yesterday	tomorrow
2	yesterday	tomorrow	**9**	yesterday	tomorrow
3	yesterday	tomorrow	**10**	yesterday	tomorrow
4	yesterday	tomorrow	**11**	yesterday	tomorrow
5	yesterday	tomorrow	**12**	yesterday	tomorrow
6	yesterday	tomorrow	**13**	yesterday	tomorrow
7	yesterday	tomorrow	**14**	yesterday	tomorrow

C. What's the Line?

Complete the following excuses.

will/won't be able to have to	was/wasn't able to has to	were/weren't able to had to	could/couldn't

1. I'm sorry that I __won't be able to__ come to your party tonight. I ___have to___ work late.

2. I'm happy my husband and I _____ come to your house for dinner next weekend. But we'll _____ leave early to pick up our daughter.

3. Henry _____ come to work early yesterday. He _____ take his car to the mechanic.

4. Mr. President, you _____ attend the press conference this afternoon. You _____ meet with the French ambassador.

5. My children _____ go to school yesterday. They _____ go to the doctor.

6. Dr. Denton _____ see you on Thursday morning because he _____ be at the hospital. But I'm sure the doctor _____ see you on Friday.

7. I'm sorry that I _____ come to the meeting yesterday. I _____ start my car.

D. Matching Lines

Which words go together?

_h_ 1. hang up   a. forgot

___ 2. have to   b. bought

___ 3. go   c. took

___ 4. forget   d. got

___ 5. get   e. had to

___ 6. take   f. said

___ 7. say   g. went

___ 8. buy   h. hung up

A. What's the Response?

Choose the correct response.

1 Joe burned himself on the stove!
   a. Tell him to press the burn!
   (b.) Tell him to put cold water on the burn!

2 What happened?
   a. My sister poked herself in the eye!
   b. Let's go to the nurse's office!

3 I hurt myself on the machine!
   a. I'll call the hospital!
   b. I'll call you!

4 You won't believe what happened!
   a. Be careful!
   b. What happened?

5 Those girls spilled tea all over themselves!
   a. I'll get the first-aid kit!
   b. You won't believe what happened!

6 That parrot talks to itself all the time!
   a. I'll call a doctor!
   b. What does it say?

7 Sam and I cut ourselves!
   a. Are you bleeding very badly?
   b. Are they bleeding very badly?

8 Did you hurt yourself?
   a. Yes. Call a first-aid kit!
   b. Yes. Call a doctor!

B. Matching Lines

Match the lines.

_e_ **1** Frank, you cut ____!   a. itself

___ **2** My husband hurt ____!   b. ourselves

___ **3** I shocked ____!   c. themselves

___ **4** My sister poked ____!   d. himself

___ **5** We spilled soup all over ____!   e. yourself

___ **6** Grandma and Grandpa talk to ____.   f. herself

___ **7** The cat hurt ____!   g. yourselves

___ **8** I'm sorry that you and your friends cut ____. h. myself

C. Listen

Listen and circle the word you hear.

1. yourself (yourselves)
2. ourselves themselves
3. myself itself
4. himself herself
5. ourselves yourselves
6. herself itself
7. himself herself
8. yourselves yourself
9. themselves himself

D. The Right Choice

Circle the correct word,

The Lin family had very bad luck yesterday. Mr. Lin went to work and had to stay late to help take inventory. Mr. Lin took a box down from a shelf, and the box hit him on the head. He hurt (herself (himself))[1], and he had to go to the doctor. He couldn't go to work today.

Mrs. Lin works in a factory. Yesterday her supervisor said to her, "Please work faster." Mrs. Lin tried to work faster, but she hurt (himself herself)[2] on her machine. They had to turn off all the power in the factory, and Mrs. Lin had to go to the hospital. She won't be able to go to work today.

Yesterday Grandma and Grandpa Lin walked to the supermarket. A car hit them and they hurt (yourselves themselves)[3]. They had to get first-aid. Grandma and Grandpa Lin have to stay home today.

Timmy and Peter Lin went to school yesterday. They went to Biology class. The teacher said, "Be careful! Don't cut (ourselves yourselves)[4]!" But Timmy and Peter weren't very careful and they cut (themselves ourselves)[5]. They'll be able to go to school again tomorrow.

At 6:00 P.M. Sally decided to help with dinner. But she burned (himself herself)[6] on the stove and spilled hot water on the dog. The dog burned (myself itself)[7] very badly and had to go to the animal hospital.

Everyone in the Lin family is at home today. They all had very bad luck yesterday!

Ask Permission to Do Something

A. Wrong Way!

Put the lines in the correct order.

____ Hmm. Well, I'm not really sure.

____ Well, in that case, of course you can leave an hour early.

_1_ Excuse me, Mr. Butler.

____ Could I possibly leave an hour early?

____ Thank you very much.

____ Yes?

____ The reason I'm asking is my daughter burned herself and I have to take her to the doctor.

B. A Good Excuse or Not a Good Excuse?

Decide if each of the following is "a good excuse" or is "not a good excuse."

		A Good Excuse	Not a Good Excuse
1	"I'm sorry I can't come to the meeting this afternoon. I have to go to the doctor."	✓	
2	"I won't be able to help take inventory tomorrow because I have to see a movie."		
3	"Could I possibly leave a half hour early? My son hurt himself at school."		
4	"I'm sorry I won't be able to finish the report. I have to buy some food at the supermarket."		
5	"Could I possibly take the day off tomorrow? My parrot is sick."		
6	"I'm really sorry I wasn't able to come in early today. My car didn't start and I had to take the bus."		
7	"I'm sorry I wasn't able to stay until the end of the meeting. I had to get home to watch the football game on TV."		

C. What Are They Thinking?

What are these people thinking? Check the most likely answer.

1

I'll finish all the work before I go home.

I'm impressed. ✔

I'm not impressed.

2

I can't finish my work because I have to play golf at 5:00.

I'm pleased to hear that. ____

I'm not pleased to hear that. ____

3

Do you think we should set up the conference room now?

This employee has initiative. ____

This employee doesn't have initiative. ____

4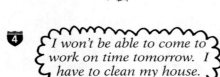

I won't be able to come to work on time tomorrow. I have to clean my house.

What an excellent employee! ____

I'm not very pleased to hear that. ____

5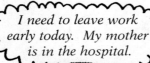

I need to leave work early today. My mother is in the hospital.

That's okay. ____

That's not okay. ____

6

Your presentation was excellent!

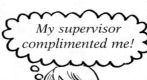

My supervisor complimented me! ____

My supervisor wasn't very pleased. ____

63

Tell What People Aren't Allowed to Do

A. Matching Lines

Match the conversations and the scenes.

a.   b.   c.   d.

e.   f.   g.   h.

___h___ **1** A. Are you allowed to swim here?
B. No, you aren't.

_____ **2** A. Are you allowed to camp here?
B. Yes, you are.

_____ **3** A. Are you allowed to play ball
here?
B. Yes, you are.

_____ **4** A. Are you allowed to ice skate
here?
B. No, you aren't

_____ **5** A. Are you allowed to park here?
B. Yes, you are.

_____ **6** A. Are you allowed to eat here?
B. No, you aren't.

_____ **7** A. Are you allowed to walk on
the grass?
B. Yes, you are.

_____ **8** A. Are you allowed to come in
here?
B. No, you aren't.

B. Listen

Are you allowed to . . . ? Listen and choose "Yes" or "No."

1 Yes (No)   **4** Yes No   **7** Yes No

2 Yes No   **5** Yes No   **8** Yes No

3 Yes No   **6** Yes No   **9** Yes No

C. Same or Different?

Are the meanings of the sentences the same or are they different?

		Same	Different
1	a. "You can't eat in the classroom." b. "You're allowed to eat in the classroom."	_____	✓
2	a. "Keep off the grass." b. "Don't walk on the grass."	_____	_____
3	a. "You aren't supposed to swim in the lake." b. "Swimming is allowed in the lake."	_____	_____
4	a. "You have to move your car." b. "There's no parking here."	_____	_____
5	a. "You can't ice skate here." b. "Ice skating is allowed."	_____	_____
6	a. "You can leave work early today." b. "You aren't allowed to leave work early today."	_____	_____
7	a. "Don't go into the meeting room." b. "You aren't allowed to enter the meeting room."	_____	_____
8	a. "Parking here is for handicapped only." b. "Handicapped people aren't allowed to park here."	_____	_____

D. Open Road!

What are you allowed to do in your English class?

| Yes, you are. | No, you aren't. | Yes, you can. | No, you can't. |

1 Are you allowed to use dictionaries? ....

2 Are you allowed to speak your native language? ....

3 Are you allowed to eat? ....

4 Can you talk to your friends? ....

5 ....? ....

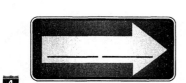

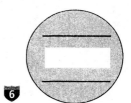

A. What's the Line?

What did the police officer say?

That sign over there.	Yes, that's right.
Do Not Enter!	Didn't you see the sign?

A. What's the matter, Officer?

B. _____ Didn't you see the sign? _____ **1**

A. The sign? What sign?

B. _____ **2**

A. What did it say?

B. _____ **3**

A. Do Not Enter?!

B. _____ **4**

A. Oh, my goodness!

B. Fill It In!

Complete the signs.

ONE WAY	NO RIGHT TURN ON RED	NO U TURN
STOP	DO NOT ENTER	NO LEFT TURN

1 NO RIGHT TURN ON RED

2

3

4

5

6

A. The Right Choice

Circle the correct word.

A. Let me see your license.

B. Here you are, Officer. What [do / **did**]¹ I [do / did]² wrong?

A. You [are / were]³ going 80 miles per hour.

B. I [am / was]⁴ going 80 miles per hour?!

A. Yes. [I'm / I'll]⁵ going to [have to / had to]⁶ give you a ticket.

B. Oh.

B. Matching Lines

Match the lines.

_g_ **1** He was driving on the wrong side of the ____.

____ **2** Don't drive through that red ____!

____ **3** You were driving 75 miles ____.

____ **4** He made an illegal ____.

____ **5** She went through a ____.

____ **6** The officer gave me a ____.

____ **7** What did I do ____?

____ **8** You were ____.

a. ticket
b. speeding
c. light
d. stop sign
e. wrong
f. per hour
g. road
h. left turn

C. Listen

Listen and put the number under the traffic violation you hear about.

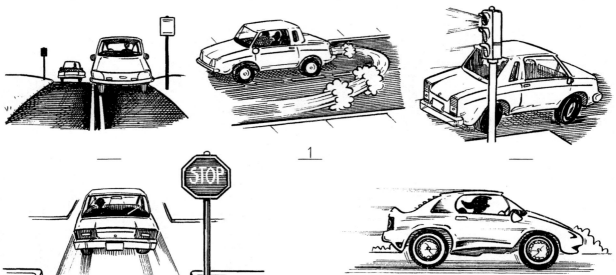

1

D. What's the Response?

Choose the correct response.

1 What were they doing wrong?
  a. They speeded.
  b. They were speeding.

2 What was I doing when you made the wrong turn?
  a. You turned on the radio.
  b. You were listening to the radio.

3 What did Margaret do wrong?
  a. She was going through a red light.
  b. She went through a red light.

4 What were you doing when I called?
  a. I was cooking dinner.
  b. I cooked dinner.

5 What were we doing when the mail came?
  a. We were watching TV.
  b. We talked on the telephone.

6 Why did Gregory get a ticket?
  a. He was going through a red light.
  b. He went through a red light.

E. Open Road!

A police officer stopped you. What did you say to each other?

A. ....

B. ....

A. ....

B. ....

A. ....

B. ....

A. What's the Word?

Complete the conversation.

rules	permitted	know	allowed	Tenants	entrance	building	leave

A. Excuse me, but I don't think you're ___allowed___ **1**
to _____ **2** your car there.

B. Oh?

A. Yes. _____ **3** aren't _____ **4** to leave
their cars at the _____ **5**. It's one of the
_____ **6** of the _____ **7**.

B. Oh. I didn't _____ **8** that. Sorry.

A. That's okay.

B. What Are the Rules?

New tenants moved into this apartment house on Main Street yesterday. Put a check next to the building rules the new tenants don't know.

RULES OF THE BUILDING

✔ You aren't allowed to cook on the balcony.

___ Don't put flowerpots on the window ledges.

___ Don't play your stereo very loudly.

___ You can't leave garbage in the halls.

___ Don't go on the roof.

___ You aren't allowed to hang laundry on the balcony.

___ Tenants aren't permitted to park in front of the entrance.

69

Deal Effectively with Housing Problems

A. The Right Choice

Circle the correct word.

A. Hello. This is Jane Fergerson in Apartment 303.

B. Yes? What can I do for you?

A. I'm wondering . . . (When) / What¹ are you going to spray our apartment?

B. Well, Ms. Fergerson, I'm very busy right now. I'm / I'll² try to spray soon.

A. You promised / promise³ to spray two weeks ago.

I'll / I'm⁴ going to have to call the Health Department.

B. Now, Ms. Fergerson. I'm sure that will / won't⁵ be necessary.

I promise I'm / I'll⁶ spray today.

A. Thank you very much.

B. Listen

What are they talking about? Listen and circle the correct answer.

1. (the heat)   the Housing Authority
2. the stereo   the TV station
3. the mess   the heat
4. the toilets   the plumbers
5. the hallway   the lead paint

6. the garbage   the superintendent
7. the car   the security deposit
8. the balcony   the security deposit
9. the hallway   the bedrooms
10. the kitchen   the Health Department

C. Crosswalk

S E C U R I T Y D E P O S I T

ACROSS

3 I promise I'll return your _____ next week.

5 When are you going to take out the _____ ?

6 You need to spray our _____ .

DOWN

1 I'll fix your stove and your _____ tomorrow.

2 Please remove the _____ from the hallways.

4 I'm going to turn on the _____ today.

D. What's the Response?

Choose the correct response.

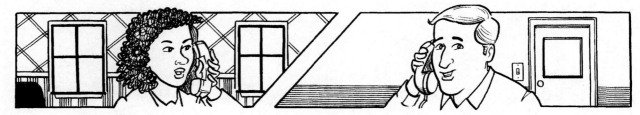

1 I'm upset! I'm going to go to court.
   a. I promise I'll return your security deposit tomorrow.
   b. Am I going with you?

2 I'm afraid I'm going to have to call City Hall.
   a. Please don't make noise after 10 P.M.
   b. I'll fix the heat today.

3 I contacted Channel 6 News yesterday.
   a. That wasn't necessary. I'll remove the lead paint today.
   b. Thank you very much.

4 I promise I'll fix your toilet soon.
   a. You promised to fix it last week.
   b. Toilets aren't permitted in the building.

A. The Right Choice

What are the rules? Circle the correct word.

There are two important rules here at the computer factory. First of all, you (must **mustn't**) go into the restricted area. Also, you (must mustn't) punch in by 7:30 A.M.

1

Before you begin your new job, I'd like to tell you about two important rules here at the Fried Chicken Shack. First of all, you (must mustn't) always wear your uniform. Also, you (must mustn't) chew gum.

2

There are two important rules here at Mike's Repairs. First of all, you (must mustn't) wear protective glasses. Also, you (must mustn't) leave the work area without permission.

3

Before you begin your new job, I'd like to tell you about two important rules here at the Flett National Bank. First of all, you (must mustn't) eat at your desk. Also, you (must mustn't) greet the customers with a smile.

4

We have some important rules here at the Ajax Corporation. First of all, you (must musn't) come to work late. Also, you (must musn't) type all of your work on your computer.

5

B. Listen

Listen and choose the correct answer.

1 a. come to work late
     (b.) punch in by 7:45 A.M.

5 a. wear your uniform
     b. ask too many questions

2 a. leave without permission
     b. leave with permission

6 a. work accurately
     b. eat at your workstation

3 a. speak politely to the customers
     b. chew gum at work

7 a. work neatly
     b. make the sundaes too large

4 a. go into the restricted area
     b. wear protective glasses

8 a. be a good employee
     b. forget to follow the rules

C. Open Road!

Officer Petrillo is a new police officer in town. Tell the new officer about some important rules of the job. Check ✔ if he must, or check **x** if he mustn't do the following.

☐ **1** Wear his police uniform.

☐ **2** Give traffic tickets.

☐ **3** Leave work without permission.

☐ **4** Greet people politely.

☐ **5** Drive on the wrong side of the road.

☐ **6** Wear protective glasses.

☐ **7** ....

D. The Right Choice

Circle the correct word.

1 My supervisor says I (can (must)) always come to work on time.

2 I'm not sure about my plans for the weekend. I (must   might) see a movie.

3 My doctor is concerned about my blood pressure. She thinks I (might   should) lose weight.

4 I'm not a good typist. I (can't   might) type very quickly.

5 You (shouldn't   can) do your homework too quickly. You (must   might) make mistakes.

6 We (mustn't   should) go into that restricted area. Employees aren't allowed to go there.

7 I'm not happy at work. I (might   shouldn't) look for a new job.

8 You (must   musn't) follow all the regulations. If you don't follow them, you (might   can't) lose your job.

A. Wrong Way!

Put the lines in the correct order.

____ The lines at the tollbooths are very long, and people are often late for work.

____ That's a good idea. I will.

____ Write to the governor?

__1__ You know . . . in my opinion, they should have more open tollbooths on this road in the morning.

____ You should write to the governor.

____ Why do you say that?

____ Yes. Really. You ought to write to the governor and express your opinion.

B. Open Road!

What should people do? Express your opinion!

PROBLEM	EXPRESS YOUR OPINION
1. The landlord won't fix my heat.	You should call the Housing Authority. You also ought to write to the city manager.
2. The bus is late every morning.	
3. A police officer gave my son a speeding ticket.	
4. The superintendent won't fix our broken steps.	
5. The landlord won't remove the lead paint in the hallway	
6. Our senator isn't doing his job very well.	

C. What's the Meaning?

Choose the sentence that has the same meaning.

1 There ought to be a law.
  a. There is a law.
  b. There should be a law. *(circled)*

2 You're allowed to speak at the town meeting.
  a. You ought to speak at the town meeting.
  b. You're permitted to speak at the town meeting.

3 The sign says "Parking for Handicapped Only."
  a. Handicapped people can park here.
  b. Handicapped people can't park here.

4 I contacted the governor
  a. I saw the governor.
  b. I called the governor.

5 Express your opinion.
  a. Say what you think.
  b. Agree with someone.

6 Tenants must have heat during the winter.
  a. It's usually cold outside during the winter.
  b. Landlords have to turn on the heat during the winter.

7 Did you know that you were speeding?
  a. Did you know that you were driving too fast?
  b. Did you know that you were driving too slowly?

8 The mayor apologized to everyone.
  a. The mayor said, "I'm sorry."
  b. The mayor agreed with everyone.

D. Likely or Unlikely?

Are the following statements "likely" or "unlikely"?

		Likely	Unlikely
1	"My doctor says I have to eat rich desserts to lose weight."	_____	✓
2	"We aren't permitted to play loud music after 11 P.M. in our building."	_____	_____
3	"I wasn't able to come to your party because I had to work."	_____	_____
4	"My supervisor is impressed because I never come to work on time."	_____	_____
5	"Our boss says we should type more carefully."	_____	_____
6	"Students must come late to class."	_____	_____
7	"The Housing Authority pays my rent."	_____	_____
8	"Our teacher says we mustn't do our homework."	_____	_____
9	"You must chew gum at work."	_____	_____

E. Listen

Listen to the conversations and choose the correct answer.

Conversation 1

1 a. This woman called a radio talk show.
  b. This woman called a TV show.

2 a. She wants the city to pick up the garbage every day.
  b. She wants the city to pick up the garbage every week.

3 a. She should write to the Housing Authority.
  b. She should write to the Health Department.

4 a. She should also call the mayor.
  b. She should also call the president.

Conversation 2

5 a. This man is going to write to the president.
  b. This man is going to call the president.

6 a. He thinks cable TV is too cheap.
  b. He thinks cable TV is too expensive.

7 a. He ought to write to the newspaper.
  b. He ought to call a talk radio program.

8 a. Also, he should write to the town meeting.
  b. Also, he should write to his congressman.

F. WordRap: *Somebody Ought To Do Something!*

Listen. Then clap and practice.

Somebody ought to write a letter.
Somebody ought to make a call.
Somebody ought to tell the landlord
There's a terrible smell in the hall!

Somebody ought to write a letter.
Somebody ought to send a fax.
Somebody ought to tell the landlord
The building is full of cracks!

Somebody ought to write a letter.
Somebody ought to make a call.
Somebody ought to tell the landlord
The ceiling's getting ready to fall!

Somebody ought to write a letter.
Somebody ought to send a note.
There's a lot of noise in Apartment 4.
I think they're building a boat!

76

Check-Up Test: Exits 4, 5, 6

A. The 5th Wheel!

Which one doesn't belong?

1	(good)	firmest	biggest	best
2	deposit	meeting	balance	withdrawal
3	well	better	neatly	accurately
4	president	senator	tenant	mayor
5	tenth	six	fourth	twentieth
6	mail	send	fax	customer
7	louder	quicker	more	faster
8	dancer	hotel	typist	painter
9	allowed	permitted	don't	okay

B. Listen

Listen and choose the correct response.

1.
 a. I suppose not.
 b. Thank you.

2.
 a. I really appreciate it.
 b. I think so, too.

3.
 a. Are you sure?
 b. Does it?

4.
 a. Yes, we do.
 b. Yes, we are.

5.
 a. Please withdraw it.
 b. Please endorse it.

6.
 a. I don't know.
 b. How much is it?

7.
 a. Certainly.
 b. Not at all.

8.
 a. Oh? Why not?
 b. Didn't you?

9.
 a. I didn't believe.
 b. What happened?

10.
 a. Yes, you do.
 b. Yes, you are.

11.
 a. I think so.
 b. I'm a fish.

12.
 a. Nothing.
 b. You're right.

13.
 a. Please fix my sink.
 b. That's a good idea.

14.
 a. There is a law!
 b. They did a law!

15.
 a. You're welcome.
 b. Why?

C. What's the Word?

Complete the sentences.

quiet	quieter	quietest

good	better	best

1. This fan is ____quieter____ than that one.

2. We need a _____ fan.

3. They bought the _____ fan.

4. It's very _____.

5. It's _____ than that one.

6. It's the _____ one.

77

D. Fill It In!

Fill in the correct answer.

1 We _____ clean the house.
   a. has to
   b. have to ⓑ

2 I _____ pay my bills.
   a. should
   b. not

3 She teaches very _____.
   a. good
   b. well

4 I can _____ the paychecks.
   a. set up
   b. give out

5 I'm sorry. They _____ work overtime.
   a. won't be able to
   b. don't do

6 She poked _____ in the eye.
   a. herself
   b. himself

7 She _____ on the wrong side of the road.
   a. did driving
   b. was driving

8 I'm sorry that I _____ come in early.
   a. shouldn't
   b. couldn't

9 Please _____ the check.
   a. endorse
   b. to endorse

10 It's _____ rain on Sunday.
   a. going to
   b. will

11 I'll give _____ the letter right now.
   a. them
   b. they

12 You're a very _____ dancer.
   a. gracefully
   b. graceful

13 Do you want me to _____ the sign?
   a. take down
   b. give out

14 My doctor says I _____ eat rich desserts.
   a. must
   b. musn't

15 They _____ fax the memo.
   a. wasn't able to
   b. weren't able to

16 Tenants _____ to put flowerpots there.
   a. aren't permit
   b. aren't permitted

17 You _____ write to the governor.
   a. ought to
   b. should to

18 Please try to work _____.
   a. good
   b. faster

E. What's the Verb?

Write the past form of the verb.

1 pay _____paid_____

2 buy _____

3 forget _____

4 make _____

5 say _____

6 hang up _____

7 write _____

8 try _____

9 cut _____

Exit 7

Discuss School Performance

Student Text
Pages
128–131

A. What's the Word?

Complete the conversation.

you	I	she	her	me

A. Hello. _____I____ **1**'m Mr. Bennett.

B. Oh! Jane's father! _____**2**'m pleased to meet _____. **3**

A. Nice meeting _____**4**, too. Tell _____**5**, how is Jane doing in Science this year?

B. _____**6**'s doing very well. _____**7** works very hard, and _____**8** grades are excellent. _____**9** should be very proud of _____**10**.

A. _____**11**'m happy to hear that. Thank you.

B. Matching Lines

What extracurricular activities do these people do?

_h_ **1** Barbara sings every day.

___ **2** Tom is in the school play.

___ **3** Carol is the class president.

___ **4** Eric likes sports.

___ **5** Alice plays the violin.

___ **6** Paul is a "literary type."

___ **7** Janet plays the trombone.

___ **8** Carla likes to study languages.

___ **9** Fred loves to study plants and animals.

a. She's in the school band.

b. He's editor of the yearbook.

c. She's in the Spanish Club.

d. He's in the drama club.

e. She's in the orchestra.

f. He's on the baseball team.

g. He's involved in the Science Club.

h. She's in the school choir.

i. She's active in the student government.

C. What's the Word?

Complete the sentences.

I	you	he	she	we	they
my	your	his	her	our	their
me	you	him	her	us	them

 We do very well in Spelling. It's __our__ favorite subject. _____ parents are very proud of _____ .

 Libby loves Math. _____ grades are excellent. _____ loves to do Math homework.

 Martha and Matt think Science is very interesting. _____ study Science every day. It's _____ best subject.

 Juan works very hard in school. History is _____ best subject. _____ enjoys learning about the presidents.

 I enjoy studying languages. This year _____'m studying French. It's _____ easiest subject, and it's _____ favorite subject.

 Bill and Bob Bentley love Physical Education. _____ go to the gym every day. Football is _____ favorite sport.

D. Listen

What are they talking about? Listen and circle the correct answer.

1. History — (French and Spanish)
2. student government — literary magazine
3. football game — student government
4. school choir — Physical Education
5. Mathematics — yearbook
6. Spelling — school orchestra
7. Science — tennis team
8. drama club — school band

Discuss School-Related Issues

A. Wrong Way!

Put the lines in the correct order.

____ She is?

____ This is Mr. Park, the school guidance counselor, calling.

____ You're welcome. Good-bye.

_1_ Hello?

____ I'm afraid she is.

____ Yes?

____ Hello. Is this Mrs. Brown?

____ Lynn is cutting some of her classes.

____ Yes, it is.

____ All right. I promise I'll speak to her about this when she gets home. Thank you for letting me know.

B. Matching Lines

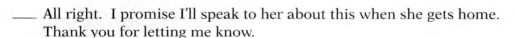

Match the lines.

_g_ **1** "We want your son to play on the soccer team."   a. Music teacher

____ **2** "We're having a meeting about college plans next week."   b. homeroom teacher

____ **3** "I'll turn on the heat soon."   c. Biology teacher

____ **4** "Did you study for the grammar test?"   d. school nurse

____ **5** "Be careful! Don't cut yourselves in this Science class!"   e. English teacher

____ **6** "Linda has to play her trombone every day."   f. guidance counselor

____ **7** "Your children are coming to school late every day."   g. coach

____ **8** "Louis has a fever. Can you come to school and pick him up?"   h. custodian

Decide Which Items Belong to People

A. The Right Choice

Circle the correct word.

1.
A. Whose skis are these? Are they (us (ours))?
B. No. They aren't (our   ours). I think they're
   Bill and (Carol   Carol's).
A. Gee, I don't think so. (Theirs   Their) are older.
B. I'll ask (theirs   them).

A. Whose notebook computer is this? Is it (yours   your)?
B. No. It isn't (me   mine). I think it's (Jane's   Janes).
A. Gee, I don't think so. (Her   Hers) is more powerful.
B. I'll ask (her   hers).

3.
A. Whose jacket is this? Is it (your   yours)?
B. No. It isn't (my   mine). I think it's (Jim's   Jim).
A. Gee, I don't think so. (His   He) is fancier.
B. I'll ask (his   him).

4.
A. Whose kittens are these? Are they (yours   your)?
B. No. They aren't (my   mine). I think they're
   the (neighbors'   neighbor).
A. Gee, I don't think so. (Theirs   Their) are cuter.
B. I'll ask (him   them).

B. WordRap: *Whose Things?*

Listen. Then clap and practice.

A. Whose dog is this? Is it Jim's?
B. No, it's not. It's Tim's.
A. Whose gloves are these? Are they Jack's?
B. No, they're not. They're Mack's.
A. Whose coat is this? Is it Ann's?
B. No, it's not. It's Fran's.
A. Whose rings are these? Are they Ellen's?
B. No, they're not. They're Helen's.

ALL: Whose things? Whose things?
     Whose things? Whose things?

A. The Right Choice

Circle the correct answer.

A. How much longer will you be studying?

B. (We'll be studying)[1]   until[2]   another hour.
    We'll studying   for

A. How much longer will I be staying here in the hospital?

B. You be staying[3]   until[4]   the end of the week.
    You'll be staying   for

A. How much longer will Grandpa be sleeping?

B. He'll be sleeping[5]   until[6]   this program is over.
    He's sleeping   for

B. What's the Question?

Complete the questions.

1 A. How much longer <u>will you be watching this program</u> ?
    B. I'll be watching this program until 10 o'clock.

2 A. How much longer _____ ?
    B. They'll be vacuuming for fifteen more minutes.

3 A. How much longer _____ ?
    B. He'll be playing ball until the school bus comes.

4 A. How much longer _____ ?
    B. She'll be practicing the violin until her violin teacher arrives.

5 A. How much longer _____ ?
    B. It'll be snowing for a few more hours.

A. What's the Response?

Choose the correct response.

1 What's new with you?
    (a.) Not much. How about you?
    b. I'm new?

2 I just won $50,000 in the lottery!
    a. That's great!
    b. I'm sorry to hear that.

3 I have some good news and some bad news. Which do you want to hear first?
    a. Pretty good.
    b. The good news.

4 Our neighbors sold their house for a lot of money.
    a. That's great!
    b. Are they upset?

5 Congratulations!
    a. What's the bad news?
    b. Thank you.

6 I have some good news.
    a. Really? What's good news?
    b. Really? What is it?

7 My husband got fired last week!
    a. That's too bad.
    b. Congratulations!

8 My wife and I are going to be getting a divorce, and my children are upset about it.
    a. I hope you can work it out.
    b. What's the bad news?

9 It's going to rain for three days.
    a. That's too bad.
    b. What is it?

10 My daughter is cutting classes every day, and she isn't doing her homework.
    a. That's wonderful!
    b. That's terrible!

B. What's the Answer?

Complete the answers.

1 Are you going to get a raise this year?   Yes, _____ I am _____.

2 Was Marie promoted?   Yes, _____.

3 Does your house have termites?   No, _____.

4 Did Mr. Grinchly raise your rent again?   Yes, _____.

5 Did Harry get another speeding ticket?   Yes, _____.

6 Are you going to have a baby?   No, _____.

7 Are your children upset you're going to be transferred?   Yes, _____.

A. Wrong Way!

Put the lines in the correct order.

___ No. What?

_1_ Did you hear the news?

___ The neighbors told me.

___ No kidding! Where did you hear that?

___ Our apartment building is going to be sold.

B. What's the Word?

Complete the sentences.

problems	baby	hurricane	promoted	strike	divorce	broke up	arrested

1. The government is having very bad financial ___problems___ .

2. Did you hear the news? The man in Apartment 5 just got _____
   by the police.

3. My sister is going to have a _____ .

4. My supervisor and his wife are getting a _____ .

5. Your secretary is going to be _____ .

6. The city bus drivers are going on _____ .

7. There's going to be a _____ this week.

8. Tim and Jennifer _____ .

C. Sense or Nonsense?

Do the following "make sense" or are they "nonsense"?

		Sense	*Nonsense*
1	I read it on the radio.	_____	✓
2	Someone saw it on the 6 o'clock news.	_____	_____
3	I overheard it in the newspaper.	_____	_____
4	My next door neighbor told me.	_____	_____
5	All the radios are whispering about it.	_____	_____

85

D. What's the Word?

Complete the following. You decide what the rumor was.

announcement	company	overheard	rumor
cafeteria	conference	whispering	read

Bob heard a ___rumor___ **1** at work last Monday.
The whole _____ **2** was talking about it.
The secretaries were _____ **3** about it in the
_____ **4**. Bob _____ **5** two custodians
talking about it in the hallway. And Bob's supervisor
_____ **6** about it on his e-mail. Was the rumor
true? Finally, the company directors said, "We're going
to make an important _____ **7** at 4:00 P.M.
in the _____ **8** room." Everybody went and
listened. The rumor was true! The company directors
announced, "..

....

...."

E. Crosswalk

ACROSS

3 I'm going to be _____ to another
city and my family is upset about it.

5 I'm afraid your son _____ a fight
in the cafeteria.

6 Kathy isn't _____ her homework.

DOWN

1 I'm upset! I _____ fifty cents in
the vending machine.

2 My husband got _____ from
his job.

4 My son wasn't _____ to medical
school.

Give Compliments

A. The Right Choice

Circle the correct word.

1 I really like your new sofa. It's very ((colorful) intelligent).

Thank you.

(Where When) did you get it?

I got it last weekend.

2 I really like your new puppy. He's very (old cute).

Thanks.

(What Why) did you name him?

I named him Rusty.

3 I really like your new sports car. It's very (flattering smooth).

I agree.

(Why When) did you get it?

I got it because I'm going through a mid-life crisis.

4 I like your new computer. It's very (comfortable powerful).

I know.

(Where Why) did you buy it?

I bought it at Computerland.

B. Matching Lines

Match the questions and answers.

__d__ **1** When did you buy it?

____ **2** How much does it weigh?

____ **3** Who cut your son's hair?

____ **4** What did you name your kitten?

____ **5** Why did you buy a motorcycle?

____ **6** Where did you get this sofa?

a. Sam at Supercuts Salon.

b. At Dave's Discount Department Store.

c. Because I really wanted one.

d. Last weekend.

e. Fluffy.

f. Two pounds.

87

Discuss Planned Activities

Student Text
Pages
144–145

A. The Right Choice

Circle the correct word.

A. **Who / (What)**[1] are you going to do on your next vacation?

B. I'm not **know / sure**[2]. I'll probably go to the mountains. How about you?

A. I don't **sure / know**[3]. I **might / maybe**[4] go to the beach, or I **might / maybe**[5] stay home and relax.

B. Well, **whenever / whatever**[6] you decide to do, I hope you enjoy yourself.

A. Thanks. **Me / You**[7], too.

B. Listen

Listen and choose the correct answer.

1. a. She's going skiing.
   b. She might go skiing.   ← circled

2. a. It's going to be nice.
   b. The weather might be bad this weekend.

3. a. He's going skydiving.
   b. He might go skydiving.

4. a. They might retire.
   b. They're going to live in Houston when they retire.

5. a. He isn't going to watch the news.
   b. He might watch the news.

6. a. Maybe she'll work at the bank.
   b. She'll be working at the bank.

7. a. Maybe they'll go on vacation.
   b. They're going on vacation.

8. a. He's going to college when he finishes high school.
   b. He might go to college when he finishes high school.

88

C. Sure or Not Sure?

Are the speakers "sure" or "not sure"?

		Sure	Not Sure
1	"I might go to a movie this weekend."	_____	✓
2	"I know I'm going to get fired."	_____	_____
3	"You aren't allowed to stand there."	_____	_____
4	"The Robinsons are going to Florida soon."	_____	_____
5	"I think it might rain tomorrow."	_____	_____
6	"I'll be working here until the end of June."	_____	_____
7	"They don't know."	_____	_____
8	"I'm positive I'm going to the senior class picnic."	_____	_____
9	"Hmm. I think I'll do my homework today. But maybe I'll go to the beach. I really don't know."	_____	_____

D. The Right Choice

Circle the correct word.

1. Dan is doing very well in school. You (might (should)) be proud of him.

We are.

2. It's going to rain this Saturday.

We (might   must) have to cancel the senior class picnic.

3. When you make a long-distance call, you (might   have to) dial "zero."

Oh. Thank you for telling me.

4. I have a terrible stomachache.

Well, you (shouldn't   might) eat so many cookies.

5. You (mustn't   must) leave those garbage bags in the hallway.

Oh. Sorry.

6. I'm upset about the pollution in our city.

You (can't   ought to) write a letter to the newspaper.

Learn How to Politely Interrupt Someone

Student Text Pages 148–149

 ## A. The Right Choice

Circle the correct word.

A. Excuse me. I'm ~~worry~~ / (sorry) ¹ to interrupt, but we need some more rice.

B. Did you say ice / rice ²?

A. No. Ice / Rice ³.

B. Oh, okay. Thank you.

 ## B. Listen

Listen and put a check next to the sentence you hear.

1 ✔ Always do your best!
___ Always wear your vest!

2 ___ Do you have the time?
___ Do you have a dime?

3 ___ Is there any pepper in the soup?
___ Is there any butter in the soup?

4 ___ Please put the bed near the table.
___ Please put the bread on the table.

5 ___ Could you tell me where the kitchen is?
___ Could you tell me where the chicken is?

6 ___ You need to take these pills.
___ You need to take these bills.

7 ___ I'd like some juice.
___ I'd like some fruit.

8 ___ Make a turn at the right.
___ Make a turn at the light.

9 ___ What was I doing wrong?
___ What was I doing for so long?

10 ___ I'm sorry, but that isn't correct.
___ I'm sorry, but that isn't collect.

C. Sense or Nonsense?

Do the following "make sense" or are they "nonsense"?

		Sense	Nonsense
1	"I like to go to the peach."	_____	✓
2	"I like to go to the beach."	_____	_____
3	"Please collect if I'm wrong."	_____	_____
4	"Please correct me if I'm wrong."	_____	_____
5	"These fries are delicious!"	_____	_____
6	"These ties are delicious!"	_____	_____
7	"Is he your cousin?"	_____	_____
8	"Is he your dozen?"	_____	_____
9	"This bathrobe is too tall."	_____	_____
10	"This bathrobe is too small."	_____	_____

D. Open Road!

Complete the conversations with words that sound the same.

1.
A. Excuse me. I'm sorry to interrupt, . . .
   but the library closes at eight.
B. Did you say ....late........?
A. No. Eight. The library closes at eight.

A. Excuse me, Joe. I'm sorry to interrupt, . . .
   but there's a problem with the kitchen floor.
B. Did you say ....?
A. No. The floor.
B. Okay. I'll be there right away.

3.
A. Excuse me, Henry. I'm sorry to interrupt, . . .
   but the boss wants to see you.
B. Did you say ....?
A. No. The boss.
B. Okay. I'll go to his office right away.

A. Excuse me. I'm sorry to interrupt, . . .
   but Larry just hurt himself.
B. Did you say ....?
A. No. Larry.
B. Okay. I'll call the doctor.

Ask for and Give Clarification

A. What Does That Mean?

Circle true or false.

1 *Our computers are down.* — That means the computers are in the basement. — True — **False**

2 *She threw in the towel.* — That means she quit. — True — False

3 *We're overbooked.* — That means there are books on all the seats. — True — False

4 *This is my treat.* — That means she's going to eat all the cake. — True — False

5 *The test results are negative.* — That means the test results are good. — True — False

6 *I'll give you a ring.* — That means he'll stop by to visit. — True — False

B. Listen

Where are they? Listen to the conversation and check the place.

1 ✔ in a park
___ in an office

2 ___ in a restaurant
___ at a lake

3 ___ in a gym
___ in a bank

4 ___ at an airport
___ at a train station

5 ___ in a doctor's office
___ in a school

6 ___ in a school
___ in a bakery

7 ___ at a concert
___ in a school

8 ___ in an office
___ in someone's house

Learn Ways to Agree with Someone

Student Text Pages 152–153

A. Matching Lines

Match the lines.

_e_ **1** It looks like a storm is coming.

___ **2** Our English teacher taught us a lot.

___ **3** The boss is in a terrible mood today.

___ **4** This movie isn't very good.

___ **5** The children don't look very healthy.

___ **6** You take too many vitamins.

___ **7** Bruce and Brenda will break up soon.

___ **8** Those pies look very good!

a. I agree. They don't.

b. I agree. They will.

c. I agree. She did.

d. I agree. She is.

e. I agree. It does.

f. I agree. They do.

g. I agree. It isn't.

h. I agree. I do.

B. What's the Response?

Choose the correct response.

1 The soup doesn't taste very good.
   a. You're right. It's cold.
   b. I know. It's in a terrible mood.

2 We should take the bus to work.
   a. I agree. The bus is very crowded today.
   b. You're right. The expressway is very crowded.

3 Our children should go to college.
   a. I agree. They shouldn't.
   b. You're right. They're very intelligent.

4 The mayor is in a terrible mood.
   a. I know. We probably shouldn't bother him.
   b. You're right. We should bother him.

5 Sam makes delicious chicken!
   a. I agree. I'd like his recipe.
   b. You're right. It tastes terrible.

6 We should have a party for our teacher.
   a. You're right. She doesn't look very healthy.
   b. I know. She taught us a lot.

7 There's going to be a hurricane soon.
   a. I know. We should leave the beach now.
   b. Okay. Let's go swimming.

8 Cutting classes isn't allowed at this school.
   a. Okay. Let's go home now.
   b. I know. Everybody has to go to class.

93

Learn Ways to Disagree with Someone

Student Text
Pages
154–155

A. Wrong Way!

Put the lines in the correct order.

____ He smiles at you all the time. Don't you agree?

____ Oh? Why do you say that?

__1__ You know . . . I think the new student likes you.

____ No, not really. I disagree.

B. Matching Lines

Match the lines.

__d__ **1** *Yesterday's test was a piece of cake.*

a. *I disagree. I think it's too cold in here.*

____ **2** *Well, I think it's time to hit the books.*

b. *Gee, I hear it isn't very popular at all!*

____ **3** *The food in the restaurant is terrible!*

c. *I disagree. I don't think he's talented at all!*

____ **4** *Everybody says this new CD is very hot.*

d. *I disagree. I thought it was difficult.*

____ **5** *I think this TV program is very interesting.*

e. *I disagree. We can think about it later.*

____ **6** *It's much too warm in the office today.*

f. *I disagree. I think it's boring.*

____ **7** *In my opinion, Gregory is a wonderful singer.*

g. *I disagree. We can study later.*

____ **8** *I think we should brainstorm right now.*

h. *I disagree. I think it's delicious.*

94

C. What's the Word?

Complete the conversations.

efficient	mood	stale	creamy	fading	nervous	strange	relaxed

1 I think I'll try meditation. I'm very ___nervous___.

2 I think these cookies are _____. They're very hard.

3 This car isn't very safe. It's making _____ noises.

4 I think this yogurt tastes just like ice cream. It's very rich and _____.

5 I think we should buy a new TV. The colors on our TV are _____.

6 The Johnsons are on vacation. They're very _____.

7 I'm in a wonderful _____ today. I just got a big promotion!

8 Janet is probably going to get fired from her job. She isn't a very _____ worker.

D. Open Road!

Do you agree or disagree with the following statements?

I agree.	You're right.	I know.	I disagree.

1 "Our English class is very interesting." ....

2 "Our classmates speak English very well." ....

3 "Students should express their opinions in class." ....

4 "Students ought to study every day." ....

5 "The students in our class like to study English." ....

A. The Right Choice

Circle the correct word.

A. By the way, what (**time** dime)**1** is it?

B. It's 4:00.

A. Oh! It's late! I've really (have to   got to)**2** go now. I (got to   have to)**3** get to class.

B. Okay. See you soon.

A. Good-bye.

A. You know, I think I should be going now. I've (got to   have to)**4** be home before dark.

B. I (could   should)**5** be going, too.

A. So (wrong   long)**6**.

B. See you (soon   noon)**7**.

B. More Right Choices

Circle the correct word.

1 I've really got to go now. I have to pick up my husband (in   **at**) 6:00 P.M.

2 You'll have your test results (by   in) a few minutes.

3 My homework will be finished (in   at) half an hour.

4 I've got to get to the supermarket (by   before) it closes.

5 I have to get to the doctor (by   in) 4:00.

6 Can you please call back (in   at) an hour?

7 I have to finish washing my car (before   by) it rains.

8 Your advisor will meet with you (before   in) fifteen minutes.

9 Marty saw the red light (at   before) I did.

10 Somebody got fired. I heard it (in   before) the cafeteria.

C. Listen

Listen and put a check next to the best way to finish the conversation.

1 ✔ It's 3:15.
___ It's Monday.

2 ___ Go?
___ Okay. See you soon.

3 ___ Good-bye.
___ Yes, you can.

4 ___ I agree.
___ Anything else?

5 ___ Thank you for saying so.
___ So long.

6 ___ Okay. Take care.
___ I'm sorry.

7 ___ Oh. That's nice.
___ Okay. I'll talk to you soon.

8 ___ Okay. Take it easy.
___ You're wrong.

9 ___ I really appreciate it.
___ No, not really. I disagree.

10 ___ Yes, I can.
___ All right. Good-bye.

D. Word Search

Find 6 ways of saying "good-bye."

```
D O N Z W (S O L O N G) S E E T T E O P
V T A K K E E Y U O I Y C A L Y I N T
D G Y B C Z W P L K J S O O N O N T A
J T K V Y U B M Z T A K E X N U I N K
T A K S C U C A L Y O J T B D J R P E
B K Y I O N C G O O D J Y V P A S S C
M E D T O U I N M A B X Z B Y I N P A
W I T C Y I P C A L L E T Y O G U J R
R T U A L R U G O O D B Y E U K B B E
S E S L O G G U S O T T Y U S U I Y U
E A E M N Y H O S U L E W S O A S Y R
E S E S H N T J V J R U G S O L O Y C
D Y I C O S E E Y O U S O O N E L T Y
Q G T V M K E S H D F G G H E Y O U I
```

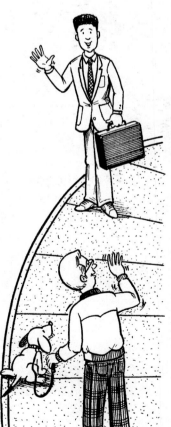

97

A. Wrong Way!

Put the lines in the correct order.

___ No, not really. I disagree. In my opinion, the chocolate shakes at Ray Roger's are more delicious.

___ Well, I'm not so sure. Why so you say that?

___ Oh? What makes you say that?

_1_ You know . . . I think the chocolate shakes at Burger Town taste better than the ones at Ray Roger's.

___ Hmm. Maybe you're right.

___ The chocolate shakes at Burger Town are sweeter. Don't you think so?

___ The chocolate shakes at Ray Roger's are more refreshing.

B. Fill It In!

Fill in the correct answer.

1 In my opinion, English is a very difficult language to learn because the spelling isn't ____.
   (a.) easy
   b. always

2 In my opinion, English is an easy language to learn because the grammar rules ____ difficult.
   a. are
   b. aren't

3 I really don't like popular music today. In my opinion, all the songs are ____.
   a. wonderful
   b. boring

4 I think today's popular music is wonderful. In my opinion, all the songs are ____.
   a. exciting
   b. terrible

5 Too much of our paycheck goes to the government. I think our taxes are too ____.
   a. low
   b. high

6 I disagree. The government needs our tax dollars. ____ our taxes are high at all.
   a. I think
   b. I don't think

7 Saving money is difficult today because ____ too many bills to pay.
   a. there are
   b. there aren't

8 I don't agree. I think it's easy to save money today because the price of food is so ____.
   a. high
   b. low

C. Listen

Listen and put a check next to the best way to finish the conversation.

1 ✔ Fine, thanks. And you?
___ I have a terrible headache.

6 ___ Okay. Good-bye.
___ How are you?

2 ___ Fine, thanks. And you?
___ I have a bad cold.

7 ___ Are you sure?
___ Okay. Bye.

3 ___ No. I think they're wrong.
___ I'm not really sure.

8 ___ So long.
___ Hello.

4 ___ Hi. How are you?
___ Good-bye.

9 ___ I agree.
___ You're welcome.

5 ___ I agree. It's great.
___ You're wrong. It's great.

10 ___ See you soon.
___ You're right. It's easy.

D. The 5th Wheel!

Which one doesn't belong?

1 I know. | (You're wrong.) | You're right. | I agree.
2 I disagree. | I know. | I'm not sure. | Why do you say that?
3 It did? | It isn't? | It wasn't? | It won't?
4 boss | computer | secretary | office assistant
5 History | football team | drama club | yearbook
6 coach | principal | father | guidance counselor

E. WordRap: *Saying Good-Bye*

Listen. Then clap and practice.

A. It's getting late.
I've got to fly.
I've got to run.
B. Good-bye. Good-bye.

A. I've got to go.
It's almost noon.
I've got to leave.
B. See you soon!

A. It's time to leave.
I have to go.
It's getting late.
B. I know. I know.

Check-Up Test: Exits 7, 8

A. What's the Word?

Complete the sentences.

my	us	your	you're	their	it	we	him

1. In __my__ opinion, it's correct.
2. Children need _____ parents.
3. What's _____ favorite subject?
4. What do _____ do?

5. Let's give _____ a promotion.
6. I know _____ going to disagree.
7. We want our raise. Give it to _____.
8. Take _____ easy.

B. Matching Lines

Match the questions and answers.

_b_ 1. Is this the boys' ball?

___ 2. Is this Jim's book?

___ 3. Is this our car?

___ 4. Is this Mom's coat?

___ 5. Is this mine?

a. Yes, it's ours.

b. Yes, it's theirs.

c. No, it isn't yours.

d. No, it isn't hers.

e. Yes, it's his.

C. What's the Response?

Write the correct response.

1. Is he doing well in school?

   Yes, ____he is____.

2. Do your children do well in Math?

   Yes, _____.

3. Will she take a shower after gym?

   No, _____.

4. Will you be here until noon?

   Yes, _____.

5. Does he have any good news?

   Yes, _____.

6. Is this your treat?

   Yes, _____.

7. Did they play on the football team?

   No, _____.

8. Was he in the school band?

   Yes, _____.

9. Are taxes too high?

   Yes, _____.

10. Did you get fired?

    Yes, _____.

11. Did you and Bill hear the news?

    No, _____.

12. Do you have any more questions?

    No, _____.

100

D. Listen

Listen and choose the correct response.

1 a. I'm happy to hear that. *(circled)*
   b. I'm sorry to hear that.

4 a. I'm happy to hear that.
   b. I'm sorry to hear that.

7 a. I'm sorry to hear that.
   b. I'm happy to hear that.

2 a. That's great!
   b. I'm sorry to hear that.

5 a. That's great!
   b. That's too bad!

8 a. That's great!
   b. That's terrible!

3 a. Congratulations!
   b. That's too bad!

6 a. Congratulations!
   b. I'm sorry to hear that.

9 a. That's wonderful!
   b. That's terrible!

E. The Right Choice

Circle the correct word.

1
~~When~~ *(circled: When)*
What
Who
did they break up?

4
Who
Why
When
got promoted?

2
Who
What
How
much longer will you be here?

5
What
Where
Which
are you going tonight?

3
When
What
Where
did you do last night?

6
Who
Which
Why
is the plane overbooked?

F. Matching Lines

Match the lines.

_d_ **1** I think we should be going now.

___ **2** Do you agree?

___ **3** What can I do to relax?

___ **4** What's your favorite subject?

___ **5** How did you hear about the strike?

___ **6** How much longer will he be on the phone?

a. You can try meditation.

b. For another half hour.

c. My neighbor told me.

d. But we just got here!

e. History.

f. No, I disagree.

Page 3

Listen and circle the word you hear.

1. You can't leave your garbage here.
2. Your brother can play here with his friends.
3. You can park your car in front of the building.
4. We can't hang our laundry on the balcony.
5. You can plant a garden in back of the building.
6. You can use the fireplace.
7. The superintendent can't come to the apartment now.
8. You can't play music after 11 P.M.
9. I can't go to the movies with you on Saturday.

Page 4

Listen and circle the word you hear.

1. A. Can I help you take out the garbage?
   B. No. That's okay. I can take it out myself.
2. A. Please hang up your laundry right now.
   B. Okay, Mom. But I can't do it by myself.
3. A. Did you put away the tables and chairs?
   B. Yes. I put them away this morning.
4. A. Can we help you clean up this mess?
   B. No, that's okay. I can clean it up myself.
5. A. Did they cut down your trees on Monday?
   B. No. They cut them down this morning.
6. A. Can you pick up those heavy bags for me?
   B. Certainly. I can pick them up for you right now.
7. A. You should put your things away.
   B. I know. I'm going to put them away right now.
8. A. Excuse me. Can I help you carry those bags?
   B. No. That's okay. I can carry them myself.
9. A. Did your husband take out the garbage?
   B. Yes. He took it out this morning.

Page 5

Listen and decide what these people are talking about.

1. Here. Let me help you carry them.
2. Thank you, but I can clean it up myself.

3. I can help you cut it down.
4. Here. I can help you take it out.
5. I can help you put them away.
6. Can I help you pick them up?

Page 7

Listen and circle the word you hear.

1. We rang your doorbell yesterday, but you weren't at home.
2. Do you have a car?
3. Bill was at school all day today.
4. On our vacation we drove through the Rocky Mountains.
5. Can you come to dinner on Friday?
6. Where did you go?
7. The Millers want to see a movie tonight.
8. I heard about the big storm on the radio.
9. Grandma and Grandpa called us this morning.
10. We were at Disneyland last week.
11. Please stop by for a visit.
12. We took the bus to Washington.
13. Do you baby-sit?
14. We went to Chicago last year.
15. You weren't in school this morning.
16. I read it in the newspaper today.

Page 9

Listen to the conversation and choose the correct answer.

A. What are you doing?
B. I'm trying to fix this radiator.
A. What's wrong with it?
B. It doesn't get hot.
A. I see. And you're trying to fix it yourself?
B. Yes. And I'm having a lot of trouble.
A. You know, maybe you should call a plumber.
B. Hmm. You're probably right.

Page 11

Listen and decide what these people are talking about.

1. It's leaking. I'm going to call a plumber.
2. It doesn't flush. We should call a plumber.
3. It doesn't get hot. Maybe we should call the superintendent.
4. We can't cook dinner because it doesn't go on. I'm going to call the gas company.
5. It doesn't close. I'm going to call a carpenter.
6. It doesn't wash the dishes. We should call a plumber.
7. We can't drive it. We should call a mechanic.
8. It doesn't get cold. We should call the superintendent.

Page 14

Listen to the conversation. Check the directions you hear.

1. A. Excuse me. Could you tell me how to make a collect call?
   B. Sure. Dial "zero." Then, dial the area code and the local number. Tell the operator it's a collect call and give your name. Have you got that?
   A. I think so. I dial "zero." Then, I dial the area code and the local number. And then I . . . hmm. Could you repeat the last step?
   B. Yes. Tell the operator it's a collect call and give your name.
   A. Okay. I understand. Thanks very much.
2. A. Excuse me. Could you tell me how to use this pay phone?
   B. Sure. Pick up the receiver. Put the money in the coin slot. Then, dial the number. Have you got that?
   A. I think so. Let me see. I pick up the receiver. I put the money in the coin slot. And then I dial the number.
3. A. Excuse me. Could you tell me how to make a person-to-person call?
   B. Sure. Dial "zero." Dial the area code and the local phone number. Tell the operator it's a person-to-person call and give the name of the person you're calling. Have you got that?
   A. I think so. I dial "zero." Then, I dial the area code and the local number. And then I . . . hmm. Could you repeat the last step?
   B. Yes. Tell the operator it's a person-to-person call and give the name of the person you're calling.
   A. Okay. I understand. Thanks very much.

Page 15

Listen and put a check next to the sentence you hear.

1. Is this Lally's Department Store?
2. Do you have any peaches?
3. Did you call at seven?
4. I fixed the train.
5. Is the museum open late?
6. I think you're right.
7. The collect call was from my brother.
8. Do you sell pears?
9. Is your name Hal?
10. Are you calling Mr. Reardon?
11. They sell gold watches.
12. What's the address on the door?
13. Please come and see.
14. Is there a problem with your earring?

Page 18

Listen and complete the train schedule.

1. The train to Atlanta leaves at 11:05 A.M.
2. A round-trip ticket to Philadelphia is $78.60.
3. The one-way fare to New York is $37.50.
4. The train to Philadelphia leaves at 4:37 P.M.
5. The one-way fare to Atlanta is $64.80.
6. A round-trip ticket to Washington is $90.75.

Page 26

Listen and circle the food item you hear.

1. A. May I help you?
   B. Yes, please. I'd like a jar of mustard.
2. A. Anything else?
   B. Yes. A pound of ground beef.
3. A. May I help you?
   B. Yes, please. I'd like a pint of chocolate ice cream.
4. A. Anything else?
   B. Yes. Two loaves of white bread.
5. A. May I help you?
   B. Yes, please. Half a pound of Swiss cheese.
6. A. Anything else?
   B. Yes. A pound of potato salad.
7. A. May I help you?
   B. Yes, please. I'd like three jars of mayonnaise.
8. A. Anything else?
   B. Yes. A bunch of grapes.
9. A. May I help you?
   B. Yes, please. Four pieces of chicken.
10. A. Anything else?
    B. Yes. Two dozen rolls.

Page 28

Listen and decide if the prices are "likely" or "unlikely."

1. A dozen hot dogs? That'll be seventeen cents.
2. A bag of potato chips? That's one twenty-nine.
3. A pound of chicken? That'll be seventy-nine dollars and ninety-nine cents.
4. A quart of milk? That'll be a dollar nineteen.
5. A jar of mustard? That'll be forty-seven fifty.
6. A dozen eggs? That'll be one cent.

Page 29

Listen and circle the correct answer.

1. I'd like a small order of . . .
2. I'll have a cup of . . .
3. I'd like two . . .
4. I'd like a roast beef . . .
5. I'd like two pieces of . . .
6. I'd like three containers of . . .

Page 30

Listen to the order and choose the correct item.

1. I'd like a large order of french fries.
2. I'll have a cup of coffee.
3. I'd like two tacos.
4. Three pieces of chicken, please.
5. I'll have an order of refried beans.
6. A chocolate shake, please.
7. I'd like a roast beef sandwich.
8. I'll have two fish sandwiches.
9. A medium Coke, please.
10. I'd like three cheeseburgers.

Page 32

Listen and circle the correct answer.

1. I'd like a glass of . . .
2. I'd prefer mashed . . .
3. I'd like lamb . . .
4. I'd like some iced . . .
5. Hmm. I think I'd like a baked . . .
6. I'm really thirsty. I'd like a . . .

Page 33

Listen and circle the correct answer.

1. Here. Have a little more . . . !
2. Do you want a few more . . . ?
3. Would you like a few more . . . ?
4. Come on! Have a little more . . . !

Page 35

Listen and put the recipe instructions in the correct order.

1. Welcome to the Friendly Gourmet Cooking Show! Today's recipe is for baked beans. First, mix together beans, onions, and ketchup. Then, put the mixture into a pan. Next, bake the mixture for four hours at 325 degrees. Serve the baked beans with hot dogs. You'll love them!
2. Welcome to the Friendly Gourmet Cooking Show! Today we're going to make orange cake. First, mix together a cup of flour, a little water, and a teaspoon of salt. Then, add a cup of sugar and a little orange juice. Next, add an egg. Put the mixture into a baking pan and bake for one hour at 350 degrees. You'll really like this orange cake!
3. Here's a wonderful recipe for mashed potatoes! First, cook the potatoes for twenty minutes. Then, mix the potatoes with a little milk and butter. Next, add a little salt and pepper. Serve with meat and vegetables.
4. Here's one of our favorite chicken recipes! First, put salt, pepper, garlic, and lemon all over the chicken. Then, put it on a rack in the oven. Next, bake it for one hour at 375 degrees. Serve it with baked potatoes and a salad. You'll really like this chicken recipe!

Page 38

Listen and circle the word you hear.

1. They bought a box of cookies.
2. I spent $10.00 at the store today.
3. I take the bus to Buffalo.
4. My husband and I sit in the park in the evening.
5. They rode on the train.
6. I had an apple for lunch.
7. We get home from work late.
8. Do the children wake up at 7:00?
9. They ate hot dogs for dinner.

Page 42

Listen to the advertisements and check the words you hear.

1. Buy a Magnabox TV! The picture on the Magnabox is the clearest and the brightest you can buy! Everybody agrees the Magnabox TV is the best!
2. Do you need a computer? Buy a McDougal today! The McDougal is more dependable than the MBI Computer. In fact, it's the most dependable and the most powerful computer you can buy. And the best news is that it's cheaper than the MBI!

Page 45·

Listen and circle the word you hear.

1. I wrote a check to University Bookstore for the textbooks.
2. I'm going to balance the checkbook today.
3. Here's a check for one twenty-five.
4. Do you remember the amount?
5. I'd like to cash this thirteen dollar check.
6. I wrote a check to Sound Studio for CDs.
7. Here's a check to pay the credit card bill.
8. The check for this month's utilities is one sixty-two fifty.
9. Did you write a check for Bill's medicine?
10. Did you remember to sign the check?

Page 48

Marcia is very busy this month. There are a lot of dates in June she has to remember. Listen and write the number of each special occasion on Marcia's calendar.

1. Her son's birthday is on June 5th.
2. Her parents' anniversary is on the 7th.
3. Marcia's daughter's graduation is on the 11th.
4. Her son's graduation is on the 15th.
5. Marcia has to remember to buy a gift for her grandmother. Her 75th birthday is on June 19th.
6. Her grandfather's birthday is on the 23rd. He'll be 82 years old!

7. Marcia and her husband have a special anniversary this month. Their 25th anniversary is on June 26th.
8. To celebrate their anniversary, Marcia and her husband are going to take a vacation trip to Greece on the 30th. What a busy month!

Page 50

Listen to the conversations and choose the correct answer.

1. A. Is there a mistake on the check?
   B. Yes. The amount isn't correct.
2. A. What's the problem with your gas bill?
   B. I was charged too much.
3. A. Did you remember to check the balance of the checking account?
   B. Yes, I did. I used a calculator.
4. A. Do you have a monthly budget?
   B. Yes, I do.
5. A. Do you write your expenses in a notebook?
   B. Yes. I know exactly how much money I can add to my savings account every month.
6. A. When is the telephone bill due?
   B. It's due on the twentieth.
7. A. I'd like to cash this check, please.
   B. All right. Please endorse it and write your account number on the back.
8. A. What's the amount of the tuition bill?
   B. Five hundred and twenty-five dollars.
   A. Five hundred and twenty-five dollars?
   B. Yes.

Page 52

Listen and circle the correct answer.

1. A. Would you like me to take down the "sale" signs?
   B. Yes. Please take them down.
2. A. Could you please call Mr. Chen?
   B. Of course. I'll call him right away.
3. A. Could you put away these dishes, please?
   B. Okay. I'll put them away right now.
4. A. Billy, could you please clean up your bedroom?
   B. Okay, Mom. I'll clean it up in a few minutes.
5. A. Please give this report to the Board of Directors.
   B. Certainly. I'll give them the report right away.
6. A. I'll be happy to hang up these announcements.
   B. Thanks. Hang them up this morning.

Page 54

Who am I? Listen and circle the correct answer.

1. You can see me on TV. People like to watch me.
2. I work at a school.
3. I speak many languages, and I work at the United Nations.
4. I work in an office.
5. I work in a factory.
6. Sometimes I work outside, and sometimes I work inside.
7. I work in a restaurant.
8. I work in a garage.
9. People watch me in the movies.
10. I interview people.
11. I study at a university.
12. People call me when there's an emergency.

Page 58

Yesterday or tomorrow? Listen and circle the correct answer.

1. I wasn't able to work overtime. I had to take my son to the doctor.
2. Bill won't be able to work this weekend. He has to attend a wedding out of town.
3. I'm happy I'll be able to see your presentation.
4. I couldn't work late. I had to pick up my car from the mechanic.
5. Betty couldn't work because she was sick.
6. I'm sorry I won't be able to help you take inventory. I have to go to my son's soccer game.
7. I won't be able to come in early. I have to go to the dentist.
8. They couldn't come to the party. They had to work.
9. Won't you be able to come to the meeting?
10. I wasn't able to cook dinner. I had to stay at work and finish the annual report.
11. Charlie won't be able to unload the shipment of new clothing. He's having problems with his back.
12. I'll be able to attend the meeting.
13. We were able to stay until the end of the meeting.
14. I couldn't set up the conference room. I had to pick up my mother at the airport.

Page 61

Listen and circle the word you hear.

1. Be careful! You're going to spill hot cereal all over yourselves!
2. We spilled hot cereal on ourselves!
3. I cut myself!
4. She hurt herself on her machine.
5. We celebrated our anniversary by ourselves.
6. There's an accident on Fourth Street! A dog hurt itself!
7. The waiter cut himself!
8. Be careful! Don't poke yourself in the eye!
9. The children hurt themselves.

Page 64

Are you allowed to . . .? Listen and choose "Yes" or "No."

1. You aren't allowed to park in front of the hospital.
2. You can fish here.
3. You're not allowed to stand in front of the white line on the bus.
4. You're allowed to camp here.
5. You can park in front of the door.
6. They're having a meeting. You're not allowed to go in.
7. There's no smoking in the movie theater.
8. Food and drinks aren't allowed in the classrooms.
9. You can't swim here.

Page 68

Listen and put the number under the traffic violation you hear about.

Officer Burton gave five traffic tickets today at the corner of Oak and Main Streets.

1. The first car made an illegal U turn.
2. The second car drove through a stop sign.
3. The third car was driving on the wrong side of the road.
4. The fourth car was speeding.
5. And the fifth car went through a red light.

Officer Burton certainly had a busy day today!

Page 70

What are they talking about? Listen and circle the correct answer.

1. I'll turn it on this afternoon.
2. I already contacted Channel 5 News.
3. Are you going to clean it up soon?
4. We'll fix them soon.
5. I'm going to remove it soon.
6. We promise we'll take it out tonight.
7. I already repaired it.
8. I'll return it next week.
9. When are you going to paint them?
10. I promise I'll spray it tomorrow.

Page 73

Listen and choose the correct answer.

1. You must always . . .
2. You must never . . .
3. You mustn't . . .
4. You must always . . .
5. You mustn't forget to . . .
6. You must never . . .
7. You must always . . .
8. You mustn't . . .

Page 76

Listen to the conversations and choose the correct answer.

Conversation 1

A. Good evening. You're on WCDN Talk Radio.

B. I'm upset. In my opinion, the city should pick up the garbage every day.
A. Why do you say that?
B. There's too much garbage everywhere. It's a mess on the streets!
A. You should write to the Health Department. Also, you ought to call the mayor.
B. Those are good ideas. I will.

Conversation 2

A. I'm going to write to the president.
B. Why?
A. Cable TV is very expensive. In my opinion, it should be cheaper.
B. You ought to write to the newspaper, too. And you should send a letter to your congressman.
A. Those are good ideas! I will.

Page 77
Listen and choose the correct response.

1. I don't think we can afford it.
2. This apartment is really noisy!
3. Channel 8 is the best TV channel.
4. We have to stop at the bank.
5. I'd like to cash this check.
6. What's the problem?
7. Could you give this memo to Mr. Jackson?
8. I won't be able to work this weekend.
9. You won't believe what happened!
10. Am I working quickly enough?
11. Are you allowed to fish here?
12. What did I do wrong?
13. What can I do for you?
14. There ought to be a law!
15. Thanks for telling me.

Page 80
What are they talking about? Listen and circle the correct answer.

1. A. Susan is very smart.
   B. I know. She's taking two languages this year.
2. A. What extracurricular activity do you do?
   B. Me? I'm the "literary type."
3. A. Are you going to the meeting?
   B. Yes. I want to hear the new senior class president talk to the class.
4. A. Does Agnes enjoy singing?
   B. Yes. She sings every day at school.
5. A. Did Mr. Small help you with your homework?
   B. Yes. I'm not having any trouble with the numbers now.
6. A. Veronica plays the violin very well.
   B. Well, you know . . . she plays every day at school.

7. A. What's your favorite subject?
   B. Biology. I love to learn about plants and animals.
8. A. Did you see the new school play?
   B. Yes. There are many talented actors in this school.

Page 88
Listen and choose the correct answer.

1. A. What are you going to do over the holiday?
   B. I'm not sure. I'll probably go skiing.
2. A. What's the weather forecast for the weekend?
   B. It's going to be sunny and warm.
3. A. Are you really going skydiving?
   B. Yes, I am!
4. A. Where are you and your husband going to live when you retire?
   B. We'll definitely be living in Houston. Our children live there.
5. A. Are you going to watch the news on TV?
   B. Probably.
6. A. What's your daughter going to do this summer?
   B. She isn't sure. She might work at the bank.
7. A. What are Grandma and Grandpa going to do for their 50th wedding anniversary?
   B. They might go on vacation.
8. A. Will your son be going to college when he finishes high school?
   B. He doesn't know.

Page 90
Listen and put a check next to the sentence you hear.

1. My mother says, "Always do your best!"
2. Do you have a dime?
3. Is there any pepper in the soup?
4. Please put the bread on the table.
5. Could you tell me where the chicken is?
6. You need to take these pills.
7. I'd like some fruit.
8. Make a turn at the light.
9. What was I doing wrong?
10. I'm sorry, but that isn't correct.

Page 92
Where are they? Listen to the conversation and check the place.

1. It's raining cats and dogs. We should go inside.
2. I'm sorry, but we're out of fish.
3. I can't balance your account now. Our computers are down.
4. I'm sorry. The flight is overbooked.
5. Mr. Jones, I'm happy to tell you the tests were negative.

6. This test is a piece of cake!
7. Jimmy, you didn't do your homework.
8. I have to leave for the office now. I'll call you when I get home.

Page 97
Listen and put a check next to the best way to finish the conversation.

1. By the way, what time is it?
2. I've really got to go now.
3. See you soon.
4. This test was a piece of cake!
5. I think I should be going now. I've got to get to my next performance.
6. I'll call you soon.
7. I've got to hang up now. The bus is here.
8. Sorry. We have to leave right now.
9. The weather this week is terrible. Don't you agree?
10. You're late! You've got to leave right now!

Page 99
Listen and put a check next to the best way to finish the conversation.

1. Hi. How are you?
2. You know . . . you don't look very well.
3. I think the government is too big. Do you agree?
4. Hello.
5. This concert is very good.
6. I'll call you soon.
7. I've got to go now. I have to pick up my children at school.
8. Have a nice day.
9. Thank you.
10. Take it easy.

Page 101
Listen and choose the correct response.

1. You should be very proud of your daughter. She's the best student in the class.
2. Your son started a fight in school this morning.
3. I was just accepted to business school.
4. The boss is in a terrible mood today.
5. My husband got fired.
6. I won a laptop computer!
7. According to my doctor, all the tests were negative.
8. Our computers are down.
9. That test was a piece of cake!

CORRELATION
ExpressWays Student Text/ExpressWays Activity Workbook

Student Text Pages	Activity Workbook Pages	Student Text Pages	Activity Workbook Pages
Exit 1		**Exit 5**	
2–3	1	88–89	51
4–5	2	90–91	52–53
6–7	3	92–93	54–55
8–9	4–5	94–95	56–57
10–11	6	96–99	58–59
12–13	7–8	100–101	60–61
14–15	9–10	102–103	62–63
16–19	11–12		
		Exit 6	
Exit 2		106–109	64–65
22–25	13–14	110–111	66
26–27	15	112–113	67–68
28–31	16–17	114–115	69
32–35	18–19	116–117	70–71
36–37	20–21	118–119	72–73
38–41	22–23	120–123	74–76
		Exit 7	
Exit 3		128–131	79–80
44–47	24–25	132–133	81
48–49	26–27	134–135	82
50–51	28	136–137	83
52–53	29–30	138–139	84
54–55	31–32	140–141	85–86
56–57	33–34	142–143	87
58–61	35–36	144–145	88–89
Exit 4		**Exit 8**	
66–69	39–40	148–149	90–91
70–73	41–42	150–151	92
74–75	43	152–153	93
76–77	44	154–155	94–95
78–79	45	156–159	96–97
80–81	46	160–163	98–99
82–83	47–48		
84–85	49–50		

TEST PREPARATION

A ASKING PERSONAL INFORMATION QUESTIONS

Choose the sentence with the same meaning.

Example:

What's your age?
- Ⓐ How tall are you?
- Ⓑ What's your weight?
- Ⓒ How old are you?
- Ⓓ Where were you born?   Ⓐ Ⓑ ● Ⓓ

1. What's your date of birth?
   - Ⓐ What country are you from?
   - Ⓑ Where were you born?
   - Ⓒ What's your marital status?
   - Ⓓ When were you born?

2. What's your marital status?
   - Ⓐ How much do you weigh?
   - Ⓑ Are you married or single?
   - Ⓒ What country are you from?
   - Ⓓ How tall are you?

3. Where were you born?
   - Ⓐ What's your height?
   - Ⓑ What's your weight?
   - Ⓒ What's your date of birth?
   - Ⓓ What's your place of birth?

4. How tall are you?
   - Ⓐ What's your height?
   - Ⓑ What's your weight?
   - Ⓒ What's your age?
   - Ⓓ What's your nationality?

5. What country are you from?
   - Ⓐ What's your marital status?
   - Ⓑ When were you born?
   - Ⓒ What's your nationality?
   - Ⓓ Are you married or single?

B ANSWERING PERSONAL INFORMATION QUESTIONS

Choose the correct answer.

Example:

What's your zip code?
- Ⓐ 415.
- Ⓑ 10027.
- Ⓒ 027-48-9451.
- Ⓓ #12-G.   Ⓐ ● Ⓒ Ⓓ

6. What's your telephone number?
   - Ⓐ 283-73-2851.
   - Ⓑ (215) 627-9382.
   - Ⓒ 97623.
   - Ⓓ 1267-B.

7. What's your height?
   - Ⓐ 155 pounds.
   - Ⓑ 27 years old.
   - Ⓒ Five feet eight inches.
   - Ⓓ Brown.

8. What's your nationality?
   - Ⓐ Mexican.
   - Ⓑ Los Angeles.
   - Ⓒ California.
   - Ⓓ Mexico City.

9. What's your weight?
   - Ⓐ 22214.
   - Ⓑ Five feet three inches.
   - Ⓒ Married.
   - Ⓓ 168 pounds.

10. What's your social security number?
    - Ⓐ 124.
    - Ⓑ 227-53-8716.
    - Ⓒ (617) 372-9106.
    - Ⓓ 33928.

1 Ⓐ Ⓑ Ⓒ Ⓓ   4 Ⓐ Ⓑ Ⓒ Ⓓ   7 Ⓐ Ⓑ Ⓒ Ⓓ   10 Ⓐ Ⓑ Ⓒ Ⓓ
2 Ⓐ Ⓑ Ⓒ Ⓓ   5 Ⓐ Ⓑ Ⓒ Ⓓ   8 Ⓐ Ⓑ Ⓒ Ⓓ
3 Ⓐ Ⓑ Ⓒ Ⓓ   6 Ⓐ Ⓑ Ⓒ Ⓓ   9 Ⓐ Ⓑ Ⓒ Ⓓ

Go to the next page >

C PERSONAL INFORMATION FORM

Name: (1)			
Street: (2)		Apartment: (3)	
City: (4)	State: (5)	Zip Code: (6)	
Social Security Number: (7)		Country of Origin: (8)	
Telephone: (9)	E-Mail: (10)	Age: (11)	
Height: (12)	Weight: (13)	Eye Color: (14)	Hair Color: (15)

Look at the information. Choose the correct line on the form.

Example:

#201-C

- Ⓐ Line 1
- Ⓑ Line 2
- Ⓒ Line 3
- Ⓓ Line 4

Ⓐ Ⓑ ● Ⓓ

11. 5479 Washington Boulevard

- Ⓐ Line 2
- Ⓑ Line 4
- Ⓒ Line 8
- Ⓓ Line 10

12. China

- Ⓐ Line 1
- Ⓑ Line 2
- Ⓒ Line 8
- Ⓓ Line 10

13. andre27@ail.com

- Ⓐ Line 1
- Ⓑ Line 6
- Ⓒ Line 7
- Ⓓ Line 10

14. 5 ft. 10 in.

- Ⓐ Line 3
- Ⓑ Line 12
- Ⓒ Line 13
- Ⓓ Line 14

15. blue

- Ⓐ Line 12
- Ⓑ Line 13
- Ⓒ Line 14
- Ⓓ Line 15

11 Ⓐ Ⓑ Ⓒ Ⓓ 13 Ⓐ Ⓑ Ⓒ Ⓓ 15 Ⓐ Ⓑ Ⓒ Ⓓ

12 Ⓐ Ⓑ Ⓒ Ⓓ 14 Ⓐ Ⓑ Ⓒ Ⓓ

Go to the next page

D GRAMMAR IN CONTEXT: Personal Information

Choose the correct answer to complete the conversation.

Example:
What's your _____?
- Ⓐ city
- Ⓑ nationality
- Ⓒ height
- ⬤ name

16. My name _____ Marie Isabel Fuentes.
- Ⓐ am
- Ⓑ is
- Ⓒ are
- Ⓓ call

17. _____ do you spell your last name?
- Ⓐ How
- Ⓑ Who
- Ⓒ Where
- Ⓓ Why

18. _____.
- Ⓐ N-A-M-E
- Ⓑ M-A-R-I-A
- Ⓒ I-S-A-B-E-L
- Ⓓ F-U-E-N-T-E-S

19. What's your _____ number?
- Ⓐ zip
- Ⓑ security
- Ⓒ e-mail
- Ⓓ telephone

20. My phone number is _____.
- Ⓐ 20018
- Ⓑ 317-29-7834
- Ⓒ (627) 442-3862
- Ⓓ #17-H

21. _____ are you from?
- Ⓐ Where
- Ⓑ When
- Ⓒ Why
- Ⓓ How

22. _____ from Guatemala.
- Ⓐ I
- Ⓑ I'm
- Ⓒ My
- Ⓓ You're

23. What's your _____?
- Ⓐ age
- Ⓑ weight
- Ⓒ height
- Ⓓ nationality

24. I'm five _____ four inches.
- Ⓐ feet
- Ⓑ pounds
- Ⓒ tall
- Ⓓ weigh

16 Ⓐ Ⓑ Ⓒ Ⓓ   19 Ⓐ Ⓑ Ⓒ Ⓓ   22 Ⓐ Ⓑ Ⓒ Ⓓ
17 Ⓐ Ⓑ Ⓒ Ⓓ   20 Ⓐ Ⓑ Ⓒ Ⓓ   23 Ⓐ Ⓑ Ⓒ Ⓓ
18 Ⓐ Ⓑ Ⓒ Ⓓ   21 Ⓐ Ⓑ Ⓒ Ⓓ   24 Ⓐ Ⓑ Ⓒ Ⓓ

Go to the next page

Look at the calendar. Choose the correct answer.

2009

January	February	March	April
May	June	July	August
September	October	November	December

Example:

Today is September 3rd. Today is _____.

- Ⓐ Monday
- Ⓑ Wednesday
- Ⓒ Thursday
- Ⓓ Saturday   Ⓐ ● Ⓒ Ⓓ

25. My birthday is March 13th. This year my birthday is on a _____.

- Ⓐ Monday
- Ⓑ Sunday
- Ⓒ Tuesday
- Ⓓ Thursday

26. My father's birthday is December 22nd. This year his birthday is on a _____.

- Ⓐ Sunday
- Ⓑ Monday
- Ⓒ Wednesday
- Ⓓ Saturday

27. I'm going to start a new job on the first Monday in May. My first day of work is _____.

- Ⓐ May 1st
- Ⓑ May 2nd
- Ⓒ May 5th
- Ⓓ May 26th

28. The twelfth day of March this year is on a _____.

- Ⓐ Wednesday
- Ⓑ Saturday
- Ⓒ Sunday
- Ⓓ Thursday

29. My sister is going to get married on the second Saturday in June. The wedding is on _____.

- Ⓐ June 7th
- Ⓑ June 8th
- Ⓒ June 14th
- Ⓓ June 15th

25 Ⓐ Ⓑ Ⓒ Ⓓ   27 Ⓐ Ⓑ Ⓒ Ⓓ   29 Ⓐ Ⓑ Ⓒ Ⓓ

26 Ⓐ Ⓑ Ⓒ Ⓓ   28 Ⓐ Ⓑ Ⓒ Ⓓ

F CLOZE READING: Providing Information About Family Members

Choose the correct answers to complete the story.

There are six people in my family. My father is am are a cashier. He
● Ⓑ Ⓒ

work works working ³⁰ in a supermarket. My mother is a an the ³¹ teacher.
Ⓐ Ⓑ Ⓒ   Ⓐ Ⓑ Ⓒ

She He It ³² works in a pre-school. My sister is with in from ³³ college. She's
Ⓐ Ⓑ Ⓒ   Ⓐ Ⓑ Ⓒ

study studies studying ³⁴ medicine. I have two brother brother's brothers ³⁵. One
Ⓐ Ⓑ Ⓒ   Ⓐ Ⓑ Ⓒ

brother is eight years old. He's in high elementary middle ³⁶ school. The other brother is
Ⓐ Ⓑ Ⓒ

sixteen years old. He's in high elementary middle ³⁷ school.
Ⓐ Ⓑ Ⓒ

G LISTENING ASSESSMENT: Giving Personal Information

Read and listen to the questions. Then listen to the interview and answer the questions.

38. What's his address?
Ⓐ 19 Reedville Street.
Ⓑ 94 Reedville Street.
Ⓒ 419 Center Street.
Ⓓ 94 Center Street.

39. When is his birthday?
Ⓐ May 3rd.
Ⓑ May 13th.
Ⓒ May 30th.
Ⓓ May 31st.

40. How tall is he?
Ⓐ 5 feet 3 inches.
Ⓑ 8 feet 5 inches.
Ⓒ 5 feet 8 inches.
Ⓓ 5 feet 10 inches.

H MONTHS, DAYS, & DATES

Look at the abbreviation. Write the correct month of the year.

NOV _____November_____	JUL _____	JAN _____
AUG _____	JUN _____	FEB _____
MAR _____	APR _____	MAY _____
SEP _____	OCT _____	DEC _____

Look at the abbreviation. Write the correct day of the week.

MON _____	FRI _____	SUN _____
WED _____	SAT _____	TUE _____
THU _____		

Write today's date. _____   **Write your date of birth.** _____

....

30 Ⓐ Ⓑ Ⓒ Ⓓ   33 Ⓐ Ⓑ Ⓒ Ⓓ   36 Ⓐ Ⓑ Ⓒ Ⓓ   39 Ⓐ Ⓑ Ⓒ Ⓓ

31 Ⓐ Ⓑ Ⓒ Ⓓ   34 Ⓐ Ⓑ Ⓒ Ⓓ   37 Ⓐ Ⓑ Ⓒ Ⓓ   40 Ⓐ Ⓑ Ⓒ Ⓓ

32 Ⓐ Ⓑ Ⓒ Ⓓ   35 Ⓐ Ⓑ Ⓒ Ⓓ   38 Ⓐ Ⓑ Ⓒ Ⓓ   [Go to the next page ⟩]

I ORDINAL NUMBERS

Write the correct ordinal number.

second	_2nd_	seventeenth	_____
ninth	_____	thirty-first	_____
first	_____	fifty-third	_____
twelfth	_____	eighty-fifth	_____

Write the correct word.

6th	_sixth_
15th	_____
21st	_____
92nd	_____

J WRITING ASSESSMENT: Personal Information Form

Fill out the form.

Name: _____

Street: _____ Apartment: _____

City: _____ State: _____ Zip Code: _____

Telephone: _____ E-Mail: _____

Height: _____ Age: _____ Date of Birth: _____ Social Security Number: _____

Hair Color: _____ Eye Color: _____ Country of Origin: _____

Signature: _____ Today's Date: _____

K SPEAKING ASSESSMENT

I can ask and answer these questions:

Ask Answer
- ☐ ☐ What's your name?
- ☐ ☐ What's your address?
- ☐ ☐ What's your telephone number?
- ☐ ☐ What's your age?
- ☐ ☐ What's your date of birth?

Ask Answer
- ☐ ☐ Where are you from?
- ☐ ☐ What's your social security number?
- ☐ ☐ What's your height?
- ☐ ☐ Who are the people in your family?
- ☐ ☐ What do they do?

Name _____

Date _____ Class _____

1b

A HOUSING ADS
Look at the classified ads for housing. Choose the correct answer.

2 BR 1 BA, d/w, $950 incl util. 273-4651.	3BR 2 BA, big apt, d/w, cac, w/d, $1400 + util. Avail 9/15. 727-4981.
1 BR 1 BA, w/w, catv, nr hospital, $750 + util. Avail 10/1. 589-7315.	2 BR 1 1/2 BA, pkg, nr airport, d/w, incl catv, $875 + elec. 863-4193.

1. You're looking for a one-bedroom apartment. Which number will you call?
   - (A) 273-4651.
   - (B) 589-7315.
   - (C) 727-4981.
   - (D) 863-4193.

2. You need an apartment with two bathrooms. Which number will you call?
   - (A) 863-4193.
   - (B) 273-4651.
   - (C) 589-7315.
   - (D) 727-4981.

3. Which apartment includes utilities?
   - (A) The 2-bedroom apartment with 1 bath.
   - (B) The 2-bedroom apartment with 1 1/2 baths.
   - (C) The 3-bedroom apartment.
   - (D) The 1-bedroom apartment.

4. Which apartment doesn't have a dishwasher?
   - (A) The 2-bedroom apartment with 1 bath.
   - (B) The 2-bedroom apartment with 1 1/2 baths.
   - (C) The 1-bedroom apartment.
   - (D) The 3-bedroom apartment.

5. Which apartment is available on Sept. 15?
   - (A) The 2-bedroom apartment with 1 bath.
   - (B) The 2-bedroom apartment with 1 1/2 baths.
   - (C) The 1-bedroom apartment.
   - (D) The 3-bedroom apartment.

6. How many of these apartments have cable TV?
   - (A) One.
   - (B) Two.
   - (C) Three.
   - (D) Four.

7. How much is the rent for the apartment near the hospital?
   - (A) $750 plus utilities.
   - (B) $875 plus electricity.
   - (C) $950 plus utilities.
   - (D) $1400 plus utilities.

8. What does the 3-bedroom apartment have that the other apartments don't have?
   - (A) Two bathrooms and a dishwasher.
   - (B) A dishwasher and central air conditioning.
   - (C) A dishwasher and a washer and dryer.
   - (D) A washer and dryer and central air conditioning.

9. You're a pilot. You and a friend are looking for an apartment. Which number will you call?
   - (A) 863-4193.
   - (B) 727-4981.
   - (C) 273-4651.
   - (D) 589-7315.

10. What does the 1-bedroom apartment have that the other apartments don't have?
   - (A) Cable TV.
   - (B) Wall-to-wall carpeting.
   - (C) A dishwasher.
   - (D) A washer and dryer.

1 (A) (B) (C) (D)   4 (A) (B) (C) (D)   7 (A) (B) (C) (D)   10 (A) (B) (C) (D)

2 (A) (B) (C) (D)   5 (A) (B) (C) (D)   8 (A) (B) (C) (D)

3 (A) (B) (C) (D)   6 (A) (B) (C) (D)   9 (A) (B) (C) (D)

Choose the correct answer to complete the conversation.

11. Is the apartment furnished _____ unfurnished?
- Ⓐ and
- Ⓑ but
- Ⓒ or
- Ⓓ with

12. It's unfurnished. _____ any furniture in the unit.
- Ⓐ Isn't
- Ⓑ There isn't
- Ⓒ Aren't
- Ⓓ There aren't

13. Is there public _____ nearby?
- Ⓐ communication
- Ⓑ location
- Ⓒ station
- Ⓓ transportation

14. Yes. There's a bus stop _____ the corner.
- Ⓐ around
- Ⓑ between
- Ⓒ next
- Ⓓ across

15. _____ is the rent?
- Ⓐ How many
- Ⓑ What does it cost
- Ⓒ How much
- Ⓓ What is the price

16. _____
- Ⓐ On the third floor.
- Ⓑ On the first day of the month.
- Ⓒ Every month.
- Ⓓ $800 a month.

17. _____ a security deposit?
- Ⓐ Are you
- Ⓑ Is there
- Ⓒ Am I
- Ⓓ Is it

18. Yes. We require one month rent in advance when you _____ the lease.
- Ⓐ sign
- Ⓑ print
- Ⓒ leave
- Ⓓ signature

19. Is the building in _____ neighborhood?
- Ⓐ a dangerous
- Ⓑ an empty
- Ⓒ an inconvenient
- Ⓓ a convenient

20. Yes. _____ many stores in the neighborhood, and _____ a school nearby.
- Ⓐ There is . . . there's
- Ⓑ There is . . . there are
- Ⓒ There are . . . there's
- Ⓓ There are . . . there are

21. Are pets _____?
- Ⓐ loud
- Ⓑ allowed
- Ⓒ may they
- Ⓓ can we

22. Yes. Dogs and cats _____.
- Ⓐ have permission
- Ⓑ is permitted
- Ⓒ are permitted
- Ⓓ are you allowed

11 Ⓐ Ⓑ Ⓒ Ⓓ	14 Ⓐ Ⓑ Ⓒ Ⓓ	17 Ⓐ Ⓑ Ⓒ Ⓓ	20 Ⓐ Ⓑ Ⓒ Ⓓ
12 Ⓐ Ⓑ Ⓒ Ⓓ	15 Ⓐ Ⓑ Ⓒ Ⓓ	18 Ⓐ Ⓑ Ⓒ Ⓓ	21 Ⓐ Ⓑ Ⓒ Ⓓ
13 Ⓐ Ⓑ Ⓒ Ⓓ	16 Ⓐ Ⓑ Ⓒ Ⓓ	19 Ⓐ Ⓑ Ⓒ Ⓓ	22 Ⓐ Ⓑ Ⓒ Ⓓ

Go to the next page ⟩

C GRAMMAR IN CONTEXT: Describing Maintenance & Repairs Needed in a Rental Unit

23. Hello. This is David Lee, the new tenant in Apartment 412. There are _____ in my apartment.

  (A) broken
  (B) a problem
  (C) many repairs
  (D) many problems

24. What's the _____?

  (A) matter
  (B) repair
  (C) problems
  (D) troubles

25. The doorbell is broken. _____

  (A) It doesn't open.
  (B) It doesn't lock.
  (C) It doesn't ring.
  (D) It doesn't close.

26. _____ And what else?

  (A) You see.
  (B) I see.
  (C) It sees.
  (D) We see.

I understand.

27. The oven doesn't light. _____

  (A) The kitchen is dark.
  (B) I can't bake.
  (C) I can't see inside the oven.
  (D) My food always burns.

28. The bathtub is cracked. _____

  (A) There's water on the bathroom floor.
  (B) The roof is leaking.
  (C) The sink is leaking.
  (D) There's water on the kitchen floor.

29. Okay. _____

  (A) Else?
  (B) Other?
  (C) Anything?
  (D) Anything else?

30. Yes. One more thing. The kitchen sink is clogged. _____

  (A) The water is too hot.
  (B) The water is too cold.
  (C) The water doesn't go down the drain.
  (D) Water doesn't come out of the faucet.

31. All right. I'll send someone to _____ everything right away.

  (A) repair
  (B) break
  (C) fixes
  (D) will fix

Thank you very much.

32. You're welcome, and I _____ for the inconvenience.

  (A) please
  (B) thank you
  (C) sorry
  (D) apologize

23 (A) (B) (C) (D)   26 (A) (B) (C) (D)   29 (A) (B) (C) (D)   32 (A) (B) (C) (D)

24 (A) (B) (C) (D)   27 (A) (B) (C) (D)   30 (A) (B) (C) (D)

25 (A) (B) (C) (D)   28 (A) (B) (C) (D)   31 (A) (B) (C) (D)

D READING: A Floor Plan

**Look at the floor plan for this apartment.
Choose the correct answer.**

33. How many bedrooms are there?
- (A) One.
- (B) Two.
- (C) Three.
- (D) Four.

34. How many closets are there?
- (A) One.
- (B) Two.
- (C) Three.
- (D) Four.

35. How many bathrooms are there?
- (A) One.
- (B) Two.
- (C) Three.
- (D) Four.

36. How many bathtubs are there?
- (A) One.
- (B) Two.
- (C) Three.
- (D) Four.

E LISTENING ASSESSMENT: Inquiring About a Rental Unit

Read and listen to the questions. Then listen to the conversation and answer the questions.

37. Where is the 1-bedroom apartment?
- (A) On the first floor.
- (B) On the second floor.
- (C) On the fifth floor.
- (D) On the sixth floor.

38. How much is the rent on the 2-bedroom unit?
- (A) $800 a month.
- (B) $800 a week.
- (C) $1,100 a year.
- (D) $1,100 a month.

39. Which pets are allowed in the building?
- (A) Dogs, cats, and smaller pets.
- (B) Cats and smaller pets.
- (C) Cats only.
- (D) Dogs only.

40. How much is the security deposit on the 1-bedroom apartment?
- (A) $800
- (B) $1,100
- (C) $1,600
- (D) $2,200

F WRITING ASSESSMENT

**Describe your apartment or home.
Write about the rooms, the building,
and the neighborhood.
(Use a separate sheet of paper.)**

G SPEAKING ASSESSMENT

I can ask and answer these questions:
Ask Answer
- ☐ ☐ How many rooms are there in your apartment or home? Describe them.
- ☐ ☐ What's your favorite room? Why?
- ☐ ☐ Tell me about your neighborhood.

---

33 (A) (B) (C) (D) 35 (A) (B) (C) (D) 37 (A) (B) (C) (D) 39 (A) (B) (C) (D)

34 (A) (B) (C) (D) 36 (A) (B) (C) (D) 38 (A) (B) (C) (D) 40 (A) (B) (C) (D) STOP

Ⓐ FAHRENHEIT & CELSIUS TEMPERATURES

Look at the thermometer. Choose the correct temperature.

Example:

84° F.
- Ⓐ 0° C.
- Ⓑ 12° C.
- ⬤ 29° C.
- Ⓓ 84° C.

1. 32° F.
- Ⓐ -32° C.
- Ⓑ 0° C.
- Ⓒ 32° C.
- Ⓓ 64° C.

2. -16° C.
- Ⓐ 9° F.
- Ⓑ 61° F.
- Ⓒ -16° F.
- Ⓓ -9° F.

3. 12° C.
- Ⓐ -12° F.
- Ⓑ 17° F.
- Ⓒ 53° F.
- Ⓓ 70° F.

Ⓑ TEMPERATURE VALUES

Choose the correct temperature.

Example:

It's very hot today. It's _____.
- ⬤ 35° C.
- Ⓑ 35° F.

4. It's very cold today. It's _____.
- Ⓐ 28° C.
- Ⓑ 15° F.

5. I have a fever. My temperature is _____.
- Ⓐ 39° F.
- Ⓑ 39° C.

6. The water is beginning to freeze. It's _____.
- Ⓐ 0° C.
- Ⓑ 0° F.

7. The cake is baking in the oven at _____.
- Ⓐ 350° C.
- Ⓑ 350° F.

8. The water is starting to boil. Its temperature is _____.
- Ⓐ 100° C.
- Ⓑ 100° F.

120 — 50
100 — 40
80 — 30
— 20
60 —
40 — 10
— 0
20 —
— 10
0 —
— 20
20 —
— 30
40 —
— 40

°F   °C

1 Ⓐ Ⓑ Ⓒ Ⓓ   3 Ⓐ Ⓑ Ⓒ Ⓓ   5 Ⓐ Ⓑ Ⓒ Ⓓ   7 Ⓐ Ⓑ Ⓒ Ⓓ

2 Ⓐ Ⓑ Ⓒ Ⓓ   4 Ⓐ Ⓑ Ⓒ Ⓓ   6 Ⓐ Ⓑ Ⓒ Ⓓ   8 Ⓐ Ⓑ Ⓒ Ⓓ

C GRAMMAR IN CONTEXT: Beginning & Ending a Telephone Conversation

Example:
Hello. This is Robert Simon.
_____ to Ms. Harris?
- Ⓐ Can I
- Ⓑ Is she there
- Ⓒ May you speak
- ⬤ May I speak

Thank you.

Yes. Please tell her that Robert Simon called.

9. Just _____. Let me see if she's here.
- Ⓐ today
- Ⓑ an hour
- Ⓒ you wait
- Ⓓ a moment

10. I'm sorry. She isn't here right now. Can I _____?
- Ⓐ give a message
- Ⓑ give you a message
- Ⓒ take a message
- Ⓓ leave you a message

11. All right. I'll _____.
- Ⓐ give the message
- Ⓑ give her the message
- Ⓒ give you the message
- Ⓓ give me the message

D READING: Telephone Directory White Pages

Look at the telephone listings. Choose the correct answer.

12. What is John Gavin Singleton's phone number?
- Ⓐ 815 267-9534
- Ⓑ 719 389-7283
- Ⓒ 815 495-8197
- Ⓓ 815 459-8197

13. What is Rajdeep Singh's telephone number?
- Ⓐ 719 387-2415
- Ⓑ 815 637-2148
- Ⓒ 815 426-3317
- Ⓓ 815 387-2415

14. What street does Brenda Singer live on?
- Ⓐ Main Street.
- Ⓑ Lake Street.
- Ⓒ Center Street.
- Ⓓ Central Avenue.

15. What town does Linda live in?
- Ⓐ Wellington.
- Ⓑ Holbrook.
- Ⓒ Willston.
- Ⓓ Hopedale.

16. What town does Dennis Singleton live in?
- Ⓐ Arlington.
- Ⓑ Wellington.
- Ⓒ Willston.
- Ⓓ Holbrook.

SINCLAIR—SINGLETON	649
SINGER Alexander 42 Lake Nor 815 427-7251	R E S I D E N C E L I S T I N G
Dennis 143 Main Arl 815 639-9148	
Tom & Brenda 1423 Central Wil 719 825-1491	
SINGH Hardeep 753 Pond Arl 815 637-2148	
Madan 2213 River Nor 815 426-3317	
R 1719 School Hol 719 387-2415	
SINGLER Linda 27 Oak Wil 719 828-4124	
SINGLETON D 819 Shore Wel 815 267-9534	
John E 238 Maple Hol 719 389-7283	
John G 12 Adams Hop 815 495-8197	

....

9 Ⓐ Ⓑ Ⓒ Ⓓ	12 Ⓐ Ⓑ Ⓒ Ⓓ	15 Ⓐ Ⓑ Ⓒ Ⓓ
10 Ⓐ Ⓑ Ⓒ Ⓓ	13 Ⓐ Ⓑ Ⓒ Ⓓ	16 Ⓐ Ⓑ Ⓒ Ⓓ
11 Ⓐ Ⓑ Ⓒ Ⓓ	14 Ⓐ Ⓑ Ⓒ Ⓓ	

E READING: Telephone Directory Government Pages

Look at the telephone listings. Choose the correct answer.

NORTHBORO TOWN OF

AMBULANCE
    Emergency Only 911
ANIMAL CONTROL 815 821-6014
BOARD OF HEALTH 815 821-6020
ELECTRIC LIGHT DEPT 815 821-6035
HIGHWAY DEPT 815 821-6040
LIBRARY 400 Main Nor 815 821-6030
PARKS & RECREATION 815 821-6018
POLICE—
    Emergency Only 911
    All Other Purposes 815 821-5000
SCHOOLS—
    Elementary—
        Eastwick 360 Main Nor 815 821-6130
    Middle School—
        Jefferson 120 Central Nor 815 821-6140
    High School–
        Lincoln 72 School Nor 815 821-6180

17. The street lamp on Hernan's street is broken. What number should he call?
    Ⓐ 911
    Ⓑ 815 821-5000
    Ⓒ 815 821-6014
    Ⓓ 815 821-6035

18. A very mean dog is running up and down the street in front of Claudia's apartment building. What number should she call?
    Ⓐ 815 821-6020
    Ⓑ 815 821-6018
    Ⓒ 815 821-6040
    Ⓓ 815 821-6014

19. The Chungs just moved to Northboro. They want to enroll their son in 10th grade. What number should they call?
    Ⓐ 815 821-6180
    Ⓑ 815 621-6140
    Ⓒ 815 821-6130
    Ⓓ 815 821-6060

20. The Hills ate at a restaurant yesterday. This morning they all have terrible stomachaches. They think the chicken at the restaurant was bad. What number should they call?
    Ⓐ 815 821-6014
    Ⓑ 815 821-6030
    Ⓒ 815 821-6020
    Ⓓ 815 821-5000

21. There's broken glass in the playground across the street from the police station. What number should you call?
    Ⓐ 815 821-6130
    Ⓑ 815 821-6018
    Ⓒ 815 821-5000
    Ⓓ 911

17 Ⓐ Ⓑ Ⓒ Ⓓ   19 Ⓐ Ⓑ Ⓒ Ⓓ   21 Ⓐ Ⓑ Ⓒ Ⓓ

18 Ⓐ Ⓑ Ⓒ Ⓓ   20 Ⓐ Ⓑ Ⓒ Ⓓ

READING: Telephone Directory Yellow Pages

Look at the telephone listings. Choose the correct answer.

▸ **Pizza**

Classic Pizza & Pasta
　　124 Main Ple.............................315 469-7750
Jimmy's House of Pizza
　　32 Western Ree.......................315 727-9123

▸ **Plants—Retail**

Flowers For You
　　1200 Central Ree......................315 727-4124

▸ **Plumbing Contractors**

AJAX Plumbing
See Our Display Ad Page 307
　　1450 Central Ree.......................315 729-4000
DUFFY & SONS
　　632 Lake Wat.............................418 274-1234
Landry Plumbing & Heating
　　27 Pine Wal...............................418 829-3600
Reliable Plumbing
　　4250 Lawson Wol.....................315 643-2121

---

22. What is the phone number of the pizza shop in Pleasantville?

  (A) 315 727-9123
  (B) 315 469-7750
  (C) 315 727-9213
  (D) 315 469-7550

23. Which town in this area has a place to buy plants and flowers?

  (A) Retail
  (B) Centerville
  (C) Remington
  (D) Reedsville

24. What's the telephone number of the plumbing company in Watertown?

  (A) 315 729-4000
  (B) 418 829-3600
  (C) 418 274-1234
  (D) 315 643-2121

25. Where is the Ajax Plumbing Company located?

  (A) On page 307.
  (B) In Remington.
  (C) On Central Ave.
  (D) 315 729-4000.

26. You live in Wallingford, and you need a plumber right away! What number should you call for the closest plumber?

  (A) 315 643-2121
  (B) 418 829-3600
  (C) 418 274-1234
  (D) 315 729-4000

---

22 (A) (B) (C) (D)　　24 (A) (B) (C) (D)　　26 (A) (B) (C) (D)

23 (A) (B) (C) (D)　　25 (A) (B) (C) (D)

Go to the next page ⟩

G GRAMMAR IN CONTEXT: Calling 911

Choose the correct answer to complete the conversations.

Emergency Operator.

Example:
I want to _____ a robbery!
- Ⓐ do
- Ⓑ catch
- ● report
- Ⓓ make

27. _____ the address?
- Ⓐ When is
- Ⓑ Who is
- Ⓒ How is
- Ⓓ What is

241 Central Avenue, Apartment 5.

28. And please tell me _____.
- Ⓐ who happened
- Ⓑ when it's happening
- Ⓒ what happened
- Ⓓ what's going to happen

29. Burglars broke into our apartment while we _____.
- Ⓐ working
- Ⓑ were working
- Ⓒ work
- Ⓓ works

Thank you.

30. Okay. We'll send a patrol car _____.
- Ⓐ right away
- Ⓑ yesterday
- Ⓒ next month
- Ⓓ every day

This is the Fairfax Emergency Center. You're on a recorded line.

31. We need _____ at 650 Main Street!
- Ⓐ an emergency
- Ⓑ a prescription
- Ⓒ a first-aid kit
- Ⓓ an ambulance

What's the emergency?

32. I think my father is having _____.
- Ⓐ a very bad cold
- Ⓑ an upset stomach
- Ⓒ a heart attack
- Ⓓ an earache

An emergency vehicle is on the way.

Thank you.

H CLOZE READING: Phone Messages

Choose the correct answers to complete the messages.

Mom [call (A)] [calls (B)] [called ●] at 4:00. She [has (A)] [have (B)] [having (C)] ³³ to work late at the

office this evening. [She (A)] [She'll (B)] [She's (C)] ³⁴ be home at about 9 PM.

Mr. Slate called [to (A)] [from (B)] [through (C)] ³⁵ the garage about your car repairs. You should call

[us (A)] [her (B)] [him (C)] ³⁶ as soon as possible.

I LISTENING ASSESSMENT: Recorded Telephone Information

Read and listen to the questions. Then listen to the library's recorded announcements and answer the questions.

37. When does the book club meet?
    - (A) On the 1st Tuesday of each month.
    - (B) On the 3rd Tuesday of each month.
    - (C) On the 1st Thursday of each month.
    - (D) On the 3rd Thursday of each month.

38. How many evening programs are there each month?
    - (A) One.
    - (B) Two.
    - (C) Three.
    - (D) Four.

39. How many hours is the library open on Wednesdays?
    - (A) 4 hours.
    - (B) 6 hours.
    - (C) 9 hours.
    - (D) 12 hours.

40. On which date will the children's story hour meet?
    - (A) March 5.
    - (B) March 12.
    - (C) March 19.
    - (D) March 26.

J WRITING ASSESSMENT

Write about how you use the telephone. Do you use the telephone for work or for school? Do you talk to family members or friends in other places? Who do you talk to? How often? (Use a separate sheet of paper.)

K SPEAKING ASSESSMENT

I can call someone and answer the phone using these expressions:

Call Answer

☐ ☐ Hello. This is _____. May I please speak to _____?
☐ ☐ _____ isn't here right now. Can I take a message?
☐ ☐ Yes. Please tell _____ that _____.

. . . .

33 (A) (B) (C) (D) 35 (A) (B) (C) (D) 37 (A) (B) (C) (D) 39 (A) (B) (C) (D)

34 (A) (B) (C) (D) 36 (A) (B) (C) (D) 38 (A) (B) (C) (D) 40 (A) (B) (C) (D)

STOP

Ⓐ FOOD CONTAINERS & QUANTITIES

Example:

We need a _____ of jam.
- Ⓐ box
- Ⓑ loaf
- ● jar
- Ⓓ bag

1. Please get a _____ of white bread.
- Ⓐ loaf
- Ⓑ bunch
- Ⓒ quart
- Ⓓ bottle

2. I'm looking for a _____ of flour.
- Ⓐ pint
- Ⓑ head
- Ⓒ loaf
- Ⓓ bag

3. I need two _____ of whole wheat bread.
- Ⓐ loaf
- Ⓑ loaves
- Ⓒ heads
- Ⓓ boxes

4. I need a _____ eggs.
- Ⓐ box
- Ⓑ twelve
- Ⓒ dozen
- Ⓓ pound

5. Please give me a _____ of cheese.
- Ⓐ can
- Ⓑ gallon
- Ⓒ pint
- Ⓓ pound

Ⓑ FOOD WEIGHTS & MEASURES: ABBREVIATIONS

6. gal.
- Ⓐ quart
- Ⓑ pound
- Ⓒ gallon
- Ⓓ ounce

7. oz.
- Ⓐ ounce
- Ⓑ quart
- Ⓒ pound
- Ⓓ pounds

8. qt.
- Ⓐ pound
- Ⓑ pounds
- Ⓒ quart
- Ⓓ quarts

9. lbs.
- Ⓐ pound
- Ⓑ pounds
- Ⓒ quart
- Ⓓ quarts

10. ounces
- Ⓐ ozs.
- Ⓑ oz.
- Ⓒ lb.
- Ⓓ lbs.

11. pound
- Ⓐ gal.
- Ⓑ qt.
- Ⓒ lbs.
- Ⓓ lb.

Ⓒ GRAMMAR IN CONTEXT: Asking About Availability & Location of Items in a Store

12. _____ any bananas today?
- Ⓐ Is there
- Ⓑ Are there
- Ⓒ There is
- Ⓓ There are

13. Yes. _____ in the Produce section.
- Ⓐ It
- Ⓑ It's
- Ⓒ They
- Ⓓ They're

14. Excuse me. _____ the milk?
- Ⓐ Have
- Ⓑ Where
- Ⓒ Where's
- Ⓓ Where are

15. _____ in the Dairy section.
- Ⓐ It's
- Ⓑ It
- Ⓒ They're
- Ⓓ They

1 Ⓐ Ⓑ Ⓒ Ⓓ   5 Ⓐ Ⓑ Ⓒ Ⓓ   9 Ⓐ Ⓑ Ⓒ Ⓓ   13 Ⓐ Ⓑ Ⓒ Ⓓ

2 Ⓐ Ⓑ Ⓒ Ⓓ   6 Ⓐ Ⓑ Ⓒ Ⓓ   10 Ⓐ Ⓑ Ⓒ Ⓓ   14 Ⓐ Ⓑ Ⓒ Ⓓ

3 Ⓐ Ⓑ Ⓒ Ⓓ   7 Ⓐ Ⓑ Ⓒ Ⓓ   11 Ⓐ Ⓑ Ⓒ Ⓓ   15 Ⓐ Ⓑ Ⓒ Ⓓ

4 Ⓐ Ⓑ Ⓒ Ⓓ   8 Ⓐ Ⓑ Ⓒ Ⓓ   12 Ⓐ Ⓑ Ⓒ Ⓓ

Go to the next page ⟩

Look at the food advertisements. Choose the correct answer.

16. How much are four heads of lettuce?
- Ⓐ $2.00.
- Ⓑ $3.00.
- Ⓒ $4.00.
- Ⓓ $8.00.

17. How much is half a pound of Swiss cheese?
- Ⓐ $17.00.
- Ⓑ $2.50.
- Ⓒ $4.25.
- Ⓓ $8.50.

18. How much are two pounds of Swiss cheese?
- Ⓐ $8.50.
- Ⓑ $17.00.
- Ⓒ $4.25.
- Ⓓ $2.00.

19. How much are four oranges?
- Ⓐ $2.00.
- Ⓑ $1.00.
- Ⓒ $8.00.
- Ⓓ $4.00.

20. How much are a dozen oranges?
- Ⓐ $1.00.
- Ⓑ $2.00.
- Ⓒ $6.00.
- Ⓓ $12.00.

21. How much are two bottles of apple juice?
- Ⓐ Free.
- Ⓑ $1.75.
- Ⓒ $6.98.
- Ⓓ $3.49.

....

16 Ⓐ Ⓑ Ⓒ Ⓓ   **18** Ⓐ Ⓑ Ⓒ Ⓓ   **20** Ⓐ Ⓑ Ⓒ Ⓓ

17 Ⓐ Ⓑ Ⓒ Ⓓ   **19** Ⓐ Ⓑ Ⓒ Ⓓ   **21** Ⓐ Ⓑ Ⓒ Ⓓ

Go to the next page ▷

Name _____ Date _____

E READING: Food Packaging & Label Information

For each sentence, choose the correct label.

SELL BY MAR 04	Keep Refrigerated	Serving Size 1 cup (240g) Servings Per Container about 2	Center Pops Up When Original Seal Is Broken
A	B	C	D

22. Do not store at room temperature.
Ⓐ Ⓑ Ⓒ Ⓓ

23. Contains 2 cups (480g).
Ⓐ Ⓑ Ⓒ Ⓓ

24. Do not purchase if safety button is up.
Ⓐ Ⓑ Ⓒ Ⓓ

25. Do not buy after this date.
Ⓐ Ⓑ Ⓒ Ⓓ

F READING: A Supermarket Receipt

Look at the receipt. Choose the correct answer.

26. How much did the eggs cost?
Ⓐ $2.69.   Ⓒ $2.10.
Ⓑ $2.00.   Ⓓ $3.00.

27. How many bottles of soda did the person buy?
Ⓐ One.   Ⓒ Three.
Ⓑ Two.   Ⓓ Four.

28. How much did the person spend on soda?
Ⓐ $2.00.   Ⓒ $1.00.
Ⓑ $3.00.   Ⓓ $6.00.

29. How much does one loaf of bread cost?
Ⓐ $1.00.   Ⓒ $3.00.
Ⓑ $2.00.   Ⓓ $6.00.

30. How much do oranges cost at this supermarket?
Ⓐ $3.00.   Ⓒ 12 for $4.00.
Ⓑ 3 for $4.00. Ⓓ 4 for $1.00.

31. How much did the person spend?
Ⓐ $473.00.   Ⓒ $22.04.
Ⓑ $2.96.   Ⓓ $25.00.

```
JUMBO SUPERMARKET #473

   LARGE EGGS        2.10
   MILK             2.69
   JAM              3.25
 2 @ $1.00
   SODA             2.00
 3 @ $2.00
   BREAD            6.00
 2 @ 2 for $3.00
   LETTUCE          3.00
 12 @ 4 for $1.00
   ORANGES          3.00

      TOTAL      $ 22.04
      TENDER     $ 25.00
      CHANGE     $  2.96

Thanks for shopping at JUMBO!
```

Look at the menu. Choose the correct answer.

SAMMY'S CAFE

SOUP				
Vegetable Soup	Cup	1.50	Bowl	2.50
Onion Soup		2.00		3.00

SALAD
Tossed Salad Small 1.50 Large 3.00

SIDE DISHES

French Fries	2.50	Carrots	2.00
Rice	3.00	Peas	2.00

ENTREES

Chicken	7.00	Spaghetti &	
Fish	8.00	Meatballs	6.50
Steak	10.00	Vegetable Stew	7.50

DESSERTS

Pie	3.50	Fresh Strawberries	4.00
Cake	3.50		

32. Julia ate at Sammy's Cafe yesterday. She ordered a bowl of vegetable soup and a large salad. How much did she pay?
   Ⓐ $3.00.   Ⓒ $5.50.
   Ⓑ $4.00.   Ⓓ $6.00.

33. Ken ordered a small salad, chicken, and rice. How much did he spend?
   Ⓐ $11.50.   Ⓒ $12.50.
   Ⓑ $12.00.   Ⓓ $13.00.

34. Sally ate a cup of onion soup, fish, and peas. How much was her bill?
   Ⓐ $11.50.   Ⓒ $13.00.
   Ⓑ $12.50.   Ⓓ $12.00.

35. Jeff had a cup of vegetable soup, steak, french fries, and carrots. How much did he spend at the restaurant?
   Ⓐ $16.00.   Ⓒ $15.00.
   Ⓑ $15.50.   Ⓓ $14.50.

36. Dora ordered a small salad, vegetable stew, and a piece of cake for dessert. What did she pay?
   Ⓐ $11.50.   Ⓒ $12.50.
   Ⓑ $12.00.   Ⓓ $13.00.

37. Ted ordered a bowl of onion soup, chicken, carrots, peas, and fresh strawberries. How much did he pay?
   Ⓐ $16.00.   Ⓒ $17.00.
   Ⓑ $18.00.   Ⓓ $17.50.

Read and listen to the questions. Then listen to the conversation and answer the questions.

38. Where is the conversation taking place?
   Ⓐ In a supermarket.
   Ⓑ In a restaurant.
   Ⓒ In a home.
   Ⓓ In a school lunchroom.

39. What is the customer going to have for an appetizer?
   Ⓐ A glass of milk.
   Ⓑ An order of rice.
   Ⓒ The baked chicken.
   Ⓓ A bowl of soup.

40. How many side orders is the customer going to have?
   Ⓐ None.
   Ⓑ One.
   Ⓒ Two.
   Ⓓ Three.

What do you usually buy at the supermarket or other food store? How much do you usually spend? Write about it on a separate sheet of paper.

I can ask and answer these questions:
Ask Answer
☐ ☐ What foods do you like?
☐ ☐ What did you have for breakfast today?
☐ ☐ What did you have for dinner yesterday?

32 Ⓐ Ⓑ Ⓒ Ⓓ	35 Ⓐ Ⓑ Ⓒ Ⓓ	38 Ⓐ Ⓑ Ⓒ Ⓓ
33 Ⓐ Ⓑ Ⓒ Ⓓ	36 Ⓐ Ⓑ Ⓒ Ⓓ	39 Ⓐ Ⓑ Ⓒ Ⓓ
34 Ⓐ Ⓑ Ⓒ Ⓓ	37 Ⓐ Ⓑ Ⓒ Ⓓ	40 Ⓐ Ⓑ Ⓒ Ⓓ

STOP

A PERSONAL FINANCES

Choose the correct answer.

Example:

This TV is _____ that one.
- Ⓐ expensive
- Ⓑ more expensive
- ● more expensive than
- Ⓓ expensive than

1. The price is too high. Do you have a _____ one?
- Ⓐ more
- Ⓑ less
- Ⓒ less cheap
- Ⓓ less expensive

2. We need some cash. Please stop at the _____.
- Ⓐ X-ray machine
- Ⓑ ATM machine
- Ⓒ post office
- Ⓓ library

3. I'd like to _____ this in my savings account.
- Ⓐ withdraw
- Ⓑ sign
- Ⓒ cash
- Ⓓ deposit

4. I want to _____ $100 from my checking account.
- Ⓐ withdraw
- Ⓑ sign
- Ⓒ cash
- Ⓓ deposit

5. Don't forget to _____ the check on the bottom line.
- Ⓐ withdraw
- Ⓑ sign
- Ⓒ cash
- Ⓓ deposit

6. My account number is _____.
- Ⓐ Jan. 7, 2009
- Ⓑ $150.00
- Ⓒ 04372 9265
- Ⓓ 4712 Central Avenue

7. I'd like to open a _____.
- Ⓐ withdrawal slip
- Ⓑ checkbook
- Ⓒ ATM machine
- Ⓓ checking account

8. I _____ my checkbook every week.
- Ⓐ sign
- Ⓑ balance
- Ⓒ deposit
- Ⓓ withdraw

9. I wrote a _____ to pay the telephone _____.
- Ⓐ check . . . bill
- Ⓑ cash . . . bill
- Ⓒ bill . . . check
- Ⓓ bill . . . account

1 Ⓐ Ⓑ Ⓒ Ⓓ   4 Ⓐ Ⓑ Ⓒ Ⓓ   7 Ⓐ Ⓑ Ⓒ Ⓓ

2 Ⓐ Ⓑ Ⓒ Ⓓ   5 Ⓐ Ⓑ Ⓒ Ⓓ   8 Ⓐ Ⓑ Ⓒ Ⓓ

3 Ⓐ Ⓑ Ⓒ Ⓓ   6 Ⓐ Ⓑ Ⓒ Ⓓ   9 Ⓐ Ⓑ Ⓒ Ⓓ

B INTERPRETING A CHECK

		1024

(1) _____

Pay to the order of **(2)** _____ $ **(3)** _____

(4) _____ Dollars

For **(5)** _____ **(6)** _____

057009345 200042534 1024

Look at the information. Where should you write it? Choose the correct line on the check.

10. Savemax Clothing Store
- Ⓐ Line 2
- Ⓑ Line 4
- Ⓒ Line 5
- Ⓓ Line 6

11. 36.40
- Ⓐ Line 1
- Ⓑ Line 3
- Ⓒ Line 4
- Ⓓ Line 6

12. Nov. 22, 2009
- Ⓐ Line 1
- Ⓑ Line 3
- Ⓒ Line 5
- Ⓓ Line 6

13. pants & belt
- Ⓐ Line 2
- Ⓑ Line 4
- Ⓒ Line 5
- Ⓓ Line 6

14. *Pedro Martinez*
- Ⓐ Line 3
- Ⓑ Line 4
- Ⓒ Line 5
- Ⓓ Line 6

15. Thirty-six and 40/100.................................
- Ⓐ Line 2
- Ⓑ Line 3
- Ⓒ Line 4
- Ⓓ Line 5

C UNDERSTANDING ATM INSTRUCTIONS

Read the ATM instruction. Choose the correct answer.

16. Enter the amount in dollars and cents.
- Ⓐ OKAY
- Ⓑ 4761
- Ⓒ $50.00
- Ⓓ ENTER

17. Choose a transaction: WITHDRAWAL
- Ⓐ Insert card.
- Ⓑ Get money.
- Ⓒ Put in money.
- Ⓓ Press ENTER.

18. Choose a transaction: DEPOSIT
- Ⓐ Put in money.
- Ⓑ Press OKAY.
- Ⓒ Get money.
- Ⓓ Insert card.

19. Enter your PIN (Personal Identification Number)
- Ⓐ $0.00
- Ⓑ $50.00
- Ⓒ 4761
- Ⓓ P-I-N

20. Balance Inquiry
- Ⓐ Choose another account.
- Ⓑ Last Deposit: $463.12
- Ⓒ Last Withdrawal: $100.00
- Ⓓ Funds available: $1,241.63

21. Do you want to make another transaction?
- Ⓐ Enter your PIN.
- Ⓑ Press YES or NO.
- Ⓒ Enter the amount.
- Ⓓ Insert your card.

· ·

10	Ⓐ Ⓑ Ⓒ Ⓓ	13	Ⓐ Ⓑ Ⓒ Ⓓ	16	Ⓐ Ⓑ Ⓒ Ⓓ	19	Ⓐ Ⓑ Ⓒ Ⓓ
11	Ⓐ Ⓑ Ⓒ Ⓓ	14	Ⓐ Ⓑ Ⓒ Ⓓ	17	Ⓐ Ⓑ Ⓒ Ⓓ	20	Ⓐ Ⓑ Ⓒ Ⓓ
12	Ⓐ Ⓑ Ⓒ Ⓓ	15	Ⓐ Ⓑ Ⓒ Ⓓ	18	Ⓐ Ⓑ Ⓒ Ⓓ	21	Ⓐ Ⓑ Ⓒ Ⓓ

Name _____   Date _____

Example:

I want to send this
_____ to Texas.
- Ⓐ postcard
- ● package
- Ⓒ letter
- Ⓓ envelope

22. Do you want to send it
_____ surface mail or
air mail?
- Ⓐ for
- Ⓑ with
- Ⓒ by
- Ⓓ from

23. _____ recommend?
- Ⓐ What does it
- Ⓑ What do I
- Ⓒ What does he
- Ⓓ What do you

24. Let's see. It weighs eight
_____ and eleven ounces.
- Ⓐ inches
- Ⓑ pounds
- Ⓒ feet
- Ⓓ miles

25. How much will it _____?
- Ⓐ cost
- Ⓑ costs
- Ⓒ send
- Ⓓ sends

26. _____ $4.50 surface mail
or $7.25 air mail.
- Ⓐ I'll cost
- Ⓑ You'll cost
- Ⓒ It'll cost
- Ⓓ They'll cost

27. _____ will it take to get
there by surface mail?
- Ⓐ How much
- Ⓑ How many
- Ⓒ How short
- Ⓓ How long

28. About ten _____.
- Ⓐ miles
- Ⓑ ounces
- Ⓒ days
- Ⓓ feet

29. I think I'll send it by
surface mail. And I'd also
like a book of first-class
_____, please.
- Ⓐ postcards
- Ⓑ stamps
- Ⓒ money orders
- Ⓓ aerogrammes

All right.

. . . .

22 Ⓐ Ⓑ Ⓒ Ⓓ   25 Ⓐ Ⓑ Ⓒ Ⓓ   28 Ⓐ Ⓑ Ⓒ Ⓓ

23 Ⓐ Ⓑ Ⓒ Ⓓ   26 Ⓐ Ⓑ Ⓒ Ⓓ   29 Ⓐ Ⓑ Ⓒ Ⓓ

24 Ⓐ Ⓑ Ⓒ Ⓓ   27 Ⓐ Ⓑ Ⓒ Ⓓ

30. I'd like to _____ this cell phone.
- (A) give
- (B) return
- (C) take
- (D) call

31. What's the _____ with it?
- (A) matter
- (B) wrong
- (C) why
- (D) what's wrong

32. _____ small enough.
- (A) They aren't
- (B) Aren't they
- (C) It isn't
- (D) Isn't it

33. Do you want to _____ it for a smaller one?
- (A) return
- (B) buy
- (C) give
- (D) exchange

34. _____ a smaller one?
- (A) You do have
- (B) Do you have
- (C) Have you
- (D) You do

35. Yes. This used to be the _____ one, but now we have a smaller one.
- (A) smallest
- (B) more small
- (C) more smallest
- (D) much small

36. Then I think _____ exchange it.
- (A) I like
- (B) you like
- (C) you'd like to
- (D) I'd like to

37. Okay. Go to the Electronics _____. Somebody there will help you.
- (A) store
- (B) furniture
- (C) department
- (D) entertainment

F LISTENING ASSESSMENT: Returning Items

Read and listen to the questions. Then listen to the conversation and answer the questions.

38. What does the person want to do?
- (A) She wants to exchange shoes and a skirt.
- (B) She wants to exchange shoes and a dress.
- (C) She wants to return shoes and a skirt.
- (D) She wants to return shoes and a dress.

39. What's the matter with the shoes?
- (A) They aren't small enough.
- (B) They aren't large enough.
- (C) They're too large.
- (D) They're too big.

40. Where is the conversation taking place?
- (A) At the Customer Service Counter.
- (B) In the Women's Clothing Department.
- (C) On the third floor.
- (D) On the fourth floor.

30 (A) (B) (C) (D)   33 (A) (B) (C) (D)   36 (A) (B) (C) (D)   39 (A) (B) (C) (D)

31 (A) (B) (C) (D)   34 (A) (B) (C) (D)   37 (A) (B) (C) (D)   40 (A) (B) (C) (D)

32 (A) (B) (C) (D)   35 (A) (B) (C) (D)   38 (A) (B) (C) (D)

Go to the next page ⟶

Name _____ Date _____

G WRITING ASSESSMENT: Bank Deposit & Withdrawal Slips
Follow the instructions and fill out the slips.

You want to deposit a check for $200.00 and $90.75 in cash in your savings account. Your account number is 9854023.

DEPOSIT SLIP	Date _____	
	CURRENCY	
Account Number	COIN	
	CHECKS	
Name		
Sign here ONLY if cash received from deposit	LESS CASH	
	TOTAL	

You want to withdraw $300.00 from your savings account. Your account number is 437226-8.

WITHDRAWAL APPLICATION	Date _____	
	CASH WITHDRAWAL	
Account Number	CHECK WITHDRAWAL	
	TOTAL WITHDRAWAL	

Signature

You want to deposit a check for $175.00 and another for $1,396.57 in your checking account. At the same time you want to take out $100.00 in cash. Your account number is 063872-9.

DEPOSIT SLIP	Date _____	
	CURRENCY	
Account Number	COIN	
	CHECKS	
Name		
Sign here ONLY if cash received from deposit	LESS CASH	
	TOTAL	

H WRITING ASSESSMENT: Filling Out a Check

Pay this bill. Fill out the check.

Metrovision
Cable TV

Cable TV Service	$24.95
Past Due	0.00
DUE NOW	**$24.95**

1024

Pay to the
order of _____ $_____

_____ Dollars

For _____   _____

057009345 200042534 1024

I WRITING ASSESSMENT: Bank Account Application Form

Fill out the application card for a checking account.

INTEREST CHECKING ACCOUNT CARD

INDIVIDUAL ACCOUNT	LAST NAME	FIRST	MIDDLE INITIAL

Signature

BEFORE SIGNING ABOVE, READ AGREEMENT ON REVERSE SIDE

RESIDENCE ADDRESS	STREET	CITY	STATE	ZIP CODE

SOC. SEC. #	DRIVER'S LICENSE OR OTHER I.D.	PHONE BUS.: RES.:

DO NOT WRITE BELOW THIS LINE

PROXY: YES ☐ NO ☐ ALPHA ☐ CODES PLACED ☐ DATE _____

J LEARNING SKILL: Steps in a Process

Put the ATM instructions in order.

_____ Choose a transaction.
_____ Take your money, your card, and your receipt.
__1__ Insert your ATM card.
_____ Enter the amount in dollars and cents.
_____ Enter your PIN on the keypad and press ENTER.
_____ Check the amount and press OKAY.

K SPEAKING ASSESSMENT

I can ask and answer these questions:

Ask Answer
☐ ☐ Where do you shop for clothing?
☐ ☐ Why do you shop there?

Ask Answer
☐ ☐ In your opinion, what's the best place to buy a TV or other home entertainment product?
☐ ☐ Why do you think so?

STOP

Name _____

Date _____ Class _____

A HELP WANTED ADS

Look at the Help Wanted ads. Choose the correct answer.

> **CASHIERS**
> FT & PT. $11/hr. Exper. pref.
> Apply in person. M-F 9am-1pm.
> Save-Mart. 2640 Central Ave.
>
> **DRIVERS**
> FT. 40 hr/wk. Excel. salary.
> Exper. req. A-1 Car Rental
> Company. Must have own trans.
> Call 714-293-4444.
>
> **OFFICE ASSISTANT**
> PT. M-F eves 6-8. Sat. 9-11am.
> Excel. typing skills req. Tip Top
> Travel. Call Sheila at 714-592-7000.
>
> **DATA ENTRY CLERK**
> FT entry-level position.
> Req. good math skills. Will train.
> Excel. benefits. Lifeco Insurance.
> Call 714-938-3350.

Example:

Which company only has a part-time job available?

Ⓐ Save-Mart.
Ⓑ A-1 Car Rental Company.
Ⓒ Lifeco Insurance.
Ⓓ Tip Top Travel.   Ⓐ Ⓑ Ⓒ ●

1. Which ad gives information about the salary?

    Ⓐ The ad for drivers.
    Ⓑ The ad for an office assistant.
    Ⓒ The ad for cashiers.
    Ⓓ The ad for a data entry clerk.

2. Victor wants to apply for a job as a driver. What does he have to do?

    Ⓐ He has to call Save-Mart.
    Ⓑ He has to call 714-938-3350.
    Ⓒ He has to call 714-592-7000.
    Ⓓ He has to call 714-293-4444.

3. How many hours per week does the office assistant work?

    Ⓐ 10 hours per week.
    Ⓑ 12 hours per week.
    Ⓒ 14 hours per week.
    Ⓓ 40 hours per week.

4. What does a person need for the job at Lifeco Insurance?

    Ⓐ Math skills.
    Ⓑ Excellent typing skills.
    Ⓒ Experience as a cashier.
    Ⓓ Transportation.

5. Which sentence ISN'T true about the jobs at Save-Mart?

    Ⓐ Experience is preferred.
    Ⓑ A person doesn't have to call first to apply for a job.
    Ⓒ Experience is required.
    Ⓓ There are part-time and full-time jobs available.

1 Ⓐ Ⓑ Ⓒ Ⓓ   3 Ⓐ Ⓑ Ⓒ Ⓓ   5 Ⓐ Ⓑ Ⓒ Ⓓ

2 Ⓐ Ⓑ Ⓒ Ⓓ   4 Ⓐ Ⓑ Ⓒ Ⓓ

Go to the next page ⟩

B GRAMMAR IN CONTEXT: Job Interview Questions About Skills & Work History

Example:

Tell me about _____ skills.
- (A) my
- ● your
- (C) its
- (D) their

7. Do you have any _____ as a cashier?
- (A) work
- (B) work experience
- (C) help wanted
- (D) experience preferred

9. Where _____ work and for how long?
- (A) you did
- (B) did you
- (C) you were
- (D) were you

6. I _____ use a cash register, and I _____ how to take inventory.
- (A) know . . . can
- (B) know . . . know
- (C) can . . . can
- (D) can . . . know

8. Yes. I _____ a cashier in my last job.
- (A) work
- (B) worked
- (C) was
- (D) am

10. I worked at the Save-Rite Market _____ two years.
- (A) for
- (B) from
- (C) during
- (D) in

C DESCRIBING A WORK SCHEDULE

Look at Maria Perdomo's work schedule. Choose the correct answer.

WORK SCHEDULE	SEPTEMBER						
	SUN	MON	TUE	WED	THU	FRI	SAT
Start	12:00 PM	8:30 AM	8:30 AM		9:15 AM	9:15 AM	7:45 AM
End	9:00 PM	2:30 PM	2:30 PM		6:15 PM	6:15 PM	4:45 PM

Example:

How many days does she work this week?
- (A) Four.
- (B) Five.
- ● Six.
- (D) Seven.

11. Which day is her day off?
- (A) Monday.
- (B) Wednesday.
- (C) Saturday.
- (D) Sunday.

12. What time does she begin work on Thursday?
- (A) 9:15 AM.
- (B) 6:15 PM.
- (C) 8:30 AM.
- (D) 12:00 PM.

13. What time does she finish work on Tuesday?
- (A) 8:30 AM.
- (B) 6:15 PM.
- (C) 4:45 PM.
- (D) 2:30 PM.

14. How many hours does she work on Friday?
- (A) Six.
- (B) Eight.
- (C) Nine.
- (D) Ten.

15. What is the total number of hours she works this week?
- (A) 35.
- (B) 40.
- (C) 48.
- (D) 50.

....

6 (A) (B) (C) (D)   9 (A) (B) (C) (D)   12 (A) (B) (C) (D)   15 (A) (B) (C) (D)

7 (A) (B) (C) (D)   10 (A) (B) (C) (D)   13 (A) (B) (C) (D)

8 (A) (B) (C) (D)   11 (A) (B) (C) (D)   14 (A) (B) (C) (D)

T28

Go to the next page ⟶

D **GRAMMAR IN CONTEXT: Calling In Sick & Late; Requesting a Schedule Change**

Ex: Hello, Ms. Pratt. This is Ted Simon. I'm afraid I _____ come to work today.
- ● can't
- Ⓑ can
- Ⓒ have
- Ⓓ can to

17. _____ feel very sick.
- Ⓐ I
- Ⓑ I'm
- Ⓒ You
- Ⓓ You're

16. What's the _____, Ted?
- Ⓐ with you
- Ⓑ sick
- Ⓒ why
- Ⓓ matter

18. Okay. _____ come to work today.
- Ⓐ Don't have to
- Ⓑ You don't have to
- Ⓒ I have to
- Ⓓ I don't have to

19. Ms. Pratt? This is Debbie Simpson. _____ be late for work this morning.
- Ⓐ I'll arrive
- Ⓑ I'm going to arrive
- Ⓒ I'm going to
- Ⓓ I'm going

20. My bus _____ a flat tire. I _____ wait for another bus.
- Ⓐ has . . . have to
- Ⓑ have . . . has to
- Ⓒ has . . . has to
- Ⓓ have . . . have to

What happened?

Don't worry about it, Debbie. I'll see you when you get here.

Excuse me, Mr. Hunter. Can I possibly change my work schedule for next week?

21. What _____ change?
- Ⓐ you want
- Ⓑ do you want
- Ⓒ you want to
- Ⓓ do you want to

22. I'd like to change my _____ to Tuesday. I have to take my children to the doctor that day.
- Ⓐ off day
- Ⓑ day off
- Ⓒ sick day
- Ⓓ weekend day

23. I understand. Yes, you have my _____.
- Ⓐ application
- Ⓑ schedule
- Ⓒ permission
- Ⓓ change

16 Ⓐ Ⓑ Ⓒ Ⓓ   **18** Ⓐ Ⓑ Ⓒ Ⓓ   **20** Ⓐ Ⓑ Ⓒ Ⓓ   **22** Ⓐ Ⓑ Ⓒ Ⓓ

17 Ⓐ Ⓑ Ⓒ Ⓓ   **19** Ⓐ Ⓑ Ⓒ Ⓓ   **21** Ⓐ Ⓑ Ⓒ Ⓓ   **23** Ⓐ Ⓑ Ⓒ Ⓓ

E AN EMPLOYEE ACCIDENT REPORT

ACCIDENT REPORT

1. Name of Employee / Injured Person		2. Job Title

3. Sex	4. Date of Birth	5. SSN

6. Day, Date, & Time of Occurrence	7. Location of Accident

8. Description of Injury (Part of body injured & nature of injury)

9. What was the accident and how did it occur?

10. Safety Equipment or Procedures Being Used at Time of Accident

11. Contributing Factors (e.g., lack of training)

12. What do you recommend to prevent this accident in the future?

13. Name & Position of Witness(es)	14. Name of Physician	15. Employee's Signature

Look at the information. Choose the correct line on the form.

24. Shipping department
- Ⓐ Line 2
- Ⓑ Line 6
- Ⓒ Line 7
- Ⓓ Line 8

25. Friday, 2/10/08, 4:15 PM
- Ⓐ Line 3
- Ⓑ Line 4
- Ⓒ Line 5
- Ⓓ Line 6

26. I broke my right foot.
- Ⓐ Line 7
- Ⓑ Line 8
- Ⓒ Line 9
- Ⓓ Line 11

27. A big box fell off the forklift and dropped on my foot.
- Ⓐ Line 7
- Ⓑ Line 8
- Ⓒ Line 9
- Ⓓ Line 10

28. Michael Fuentes, stock clerk
- Ⓐ Line 1
- Ⓑ Line 2
- Ⓒ Line 10
- Ⓓ Line 13

29. The company should buy stronger protective shoes for employees in the shipping department.
- Ⓐ Line 12
- Ⓑ Line 11
- Ⓒ Line 10
- Ⓓ Line 9

24 Ⓐ Ⓑ Ⓒ Ⓓ   26 Ⓐ Ⓑ Ⓒ Ⓓ   28 Ⓐ Ⓑ Ⓒ Ⓓ

25 Ⓐ Ⓑ Ⓒ Ⓓ   27 Ⓐ Ⓑ Ⓒ Ⓓ   29 Ⓐ Ⓑ Ⓒ Ⓓ

T30

Go to the next page ▷

F READING: A Paycheck Stub

APRIL COMPANY		RIZAL, J.		EMP. NO. 60159

PAY PERIOD ENDING	RATE	HOURS	EARNINGS
120508	9.97	40	398.80

FED TAX	33.59	EARNINGS	398.80
FICA/MED	26.47	TAXES	70.92
STATE TAX	10.86	DEDUCTIONS	43.16
HEALTH	43.16		
		NET PAY	284.72

APRIL COMPANY   CHECK NO. 16889
                                                 DATE ISSUED 121808

Pay to   JOSE RIZAL $284.72
TWO HUNDRED EIGHTY-FOUR DOLLARS AND SEVENTY-TWO CENTS

Dee Boss

Look at the paycheck stub. Choose the correct answer.

30. What is Mr. Rizal's salary?
- Ⓐ 40 hours a week.
- Ⓑ $9.97 per hour.
- Ⓒ $284.72 per year.
- Ⓓ $398.80 per year.

31. How much did he earn during this pay period?
- Ⓐ $398.80.
- Ⓑ $9.97.
- Ⓒ $40.00.
- Ⓓ $284.72.

32. How much was the deduction for state taxes?
- Ⓐ $43.16.
- Ⓑ $33.59.
- Ⓒ $26.47.
- Ⓓ $10.86.

33. How much pay did Mr. Rizal take home after deductions?
- Ⓐ $398.80.
- Ⓑ $284.72.
- Ⓒ $40 per hour.
- Ⓓ $9.97 per hour.

G CLOZE READING: Nonverbal Behavior at the Job Interview

Choose the correct answers to complete the story.

The information you give at a job interview is important, but your nonverbal behavior is also important. You should dress [neat (A) / **neatly** ● / sloppily (C)]. Shake hands [to (A) / with (B) / for (C)] [34] the interviewer firmly. A firm handshake shows that you are [friend (A) / friends (B) / friendly (C)] [35] and confident. Make "eye contact." Look at the interviewer [direct (A) / directly (B) / director (C)] [36]. Don't speak too quickly, and don't speak too loudly or too [softly (A) / softer (B) / soft (C)] [37]. And don't forget to smile!

....

30 Ⓐ Ⓑ Ⓒ Ⓓ	33 Ⓐ Ⓑ Ⓒ Ⓓ	36 Ⓐ Ⓑ Ⓒ Ⓓ
31 Ⓐ Ⓑ Ⓒ Ⓓ	34 Ⓐ Ⓑ Ⓒ Ⓓ	37 Ⓐ Ⓑ Ⓒ Ⓓ
32 Ⓐ Ⓑ Ⓒ Ⓓ	35 Ⓐ Ⓑ Ⓒ Ⓓ	

Go to the next page ⟶

H LISTENING ASSESSMENT: A Job Interview

Read and listen to the questions. Then listen to the conversation and answer the questions.

38. What kind of position is the person applying for?
- (A) A job as a cashier.
- (B) An office position.
- (C) A position in a supermarket.
- (D) A job in a computer factory.

39. Where is the conversation taking place?
- (A) At the Larsen Real Estate Agency.
- (B) At the Citywide Supermarket.
- (C) At Landmark Data Management.
- (D) At the Johnson Insurance Company.

40. How many years of work experience does the applicant have?
- (A) 1 year.
- (B) 2 years.
- (C) 3 years.
- (D) 6 years.

I WRITING: A Job Application Form

Complete this form about yourself.

APPLICATION FOR EMPLOYMENT

Name _____ Social Security Number _____

Address _____
         Street   City   State   ZIP Code

Phone No. ( ) _____ Age (if under 21) _____ Birth Date (if under 21) ___/___/___
                                                                                Month Day Year

Position Desired _____ Salary Desired _____ Date you can start _____

EDUCATION

Type of School	Name	Location	Years Completed	Graduated?
High School				
College				
Other				

EMPLOYMENT (Start with present or most recent employer)

Date (Month/Year)	Name and Address of Employer	Position	Salary
From To			
From To			
From To			

Date _____   Signature _____

J SPEAKING ASSESSMENT

I can ask and answer these questions:

Ask Answer
- ☐ ☐ What kind of job are you looking for?
- ☐ ☐ Tell me about your skills and abilities.
- ☐ ☐ Tell me about your previous education.
- ☐ ☐ Tell me a little about yourself.

Ask Answer
- ☐ ☐ Are you currently employed?
- ☐ ☐ Tell me about your work history.
- ☐ ☐ Why do you want to work here?
- ☐ ☐ Do you have any questions about the position?

6

A FIRST-AID KIT

Choose the correct answer.

Example:

He took _____ for his headache.
- Ⓐ a cotton ball
- ● aspirin
- Ⓒ a band-aid
- Ⓓ adhesive tape

1. I cut my finger. Could you please get _____ from the first-aid kit?
- Ⓐ a band-aid
- Ⓑ a piece of paper
- Ⓒ a cotton ball
- Ⓓ an ACE bandage

2. You should put some _____ on that cut.
- Ⓐ ice cream
- Ⓑ toothpaste
- Ⓒ aspirin
- Ⓓ antibiotic ointment

3. I'm going to clean the wound with _____.
- Ⓐ adhesive tape
- Ⓑ a napkin
- Ⓒ an antiseptic cleansing wipe
- Ⓓ a band-aid

4. The doctor used _____ to take the splinter out of my finger.
- Ⓐ a knife
- Ⓑ a screwdriver
- Ⓒ scissors
- Ⓓ tweezers

5. The school nurse wrapped my ankle with _____.
- Ⓐ an ACE bandage
- Ⓑ adhesive tape
- Ⓒ toilet paper
- Ⓓ an antiseptic cleansing wipe

6. You scraped your knee. I'm going to put on _____.
- Ⓐ adhesive tape
- Ⓑ a sterile gauze dressing pad
- Ⓒ a cotton ball
- Ⓓ an ACE bandage

7. Attach the gauze pad with _____.
- Ⓐ adhesive tape
- Ⓑ an ACE bandage
- Ⓒ a string
- Ⓓ a band-aid

....

1 Ⓐ Ⓑ Ⓒ Ⓓ   3 Ⓐ Ⓑ Ⓒ Ⓓ   5 Ⓐ Ⓑ Ⓒ Ⓓ   7 Ⓐ Ⓑ Ⓒ Ⓓ

2 Ⓐ Ⓑ Ⓒ Ⓓ   4 Ⓐ Ⓑ Ⓒ Ⓓ   6 Ⓐ Ⓑ Ⓒ Ⓓ

B HIGHWAY & TRAFFIC SIGNS & SYMBOLS

Choose the correct sign.

A

C

B

D

Example:

There are train tracks ahead. Watch out for trains.

Ⓐ Ⓑ ● Ⓓ

8. No left turn.

Ⓐ Ⓑ Ⓒ Ⓓ

9. There's a crosswalk ahead. Watch out for pedestrians.

Ⓐ Ⓑ Ⓒ Ⓓ

10. When you enter this road, let the other cars already on the road go first.

Ⓐ Ⓑ Ⓒ Ⓓ

C POLICE COMMANDS & TRAFFIC SIGNS

Choose the correct sign.

A

C

B

D

Example:

"Stop! You can't enter this street from here!"

Ⓐ Ⓑ Ⓒ ●

11. "Slow down! You're in a school zone!"

Ⓐ Ⓑ Ⓒ Ⓓ

12. "You can't make a U-turn here!"

Ⓐ Ⓑ Ⓒ Ⓓ

13. "Turn around! You're going in the wrong direction!"

Ⓐ Ⓑ Ⓒ Ⓓ

Name _____ Date _____

D GRAMMAR IN CONTEXT: Describing a Suspect's Physical Characteristics to the Police

Can you describe his height?

Example:
He was about six feet _____.
- Ⓐ long
- Ⓑ high
- ● tall
- Ⓓ height

14. What was his _____?
- Ⓐ with
- Ⓑ width
- Ⓒ wait
- Ⓓ weight

15. He weighed about 160 _____.
- Ⓐ pounds
- Ⓑ feet
- Ⓒ inches
- Ⓓ yards

16. What _____ was his hair?
- Ⓐ length
- Ⓑ color
- Ⓒ look
- Ⓓ weight

17. It was dark _____.
- Ⓐ thin
- Ⓑ short
- Ⓒ long
- Ⓓ brown

18. Can you describe his _____?
- Ⓐ wear
- Ⓑ wearing
- Ⓒ clothing
- Ⓓ wore

19. He was wearing a red _____ and a pair of gray _____.
- Ⓐ pants . . . shoes
- Ⓑ pants . . . shirt
- Ⓒ shirt . . . pants
- Ⓓ shoes . . . socks

E READING: Warning Labels on Household Products

Choose the correct warning label for each instruction.

Do not use with other household chemicals.	Avoid direct contact. Wear rubber gloves.	Harmful if swallowed.	Avoid prolonged breathing of vapors.
A	B	C	D

Example:

Do not eat or drink.
Ⓐ Ⓑ ● Ⓓ

20. Do not get on skin.
Ⓐ Ⓑ Ⓒ Ⓓ

21. Use only in well-ventilated areas. Avoid fumes.
Ⓐ Ⓑ Ⓒ Ⓓ

22. Do not mix together with other products.
Ⓐ Ⓑ Ⓒ Ⓓ

··

Read the safety posters. Then answer the questions.

Duck, Cover, & Hold!
What to Do At School During an Earthquake

IN A CLASSROOM:

Duck! Get down under a desk or table. (Don't go near windows, bookcases, or other tall furniture.)

Cover! Cover your head with the desk or table. Cover your eyes. (Put your face into your arm.)

Hold! Hold on to the desk or table so it stays over your head. (Furniture can move during an earthquake.)

IN THE HALL:

Drop! Sit on the floor near an inside wall. Get down on your knees. Lean over to rest on your elbows. Put your hands together behind your neck. Put your face down.

OUTSIDE:

Don't go near buildings or walls. Sit down, or use the "Drop" position.

Stop, Drop, Cover, & Roll!
What to Do If Your Clothing Is on Fire

Stop! Stop where you are. Don't run.

Drop! Drop to the ground.

Cover! Cover your face.

Roll! Roll from side to side, over and over, until the fire goes out.

---

23. Mr. Gardner's English class had an earthquake drill in their classroom today. What did the students do first?

Ⓐ They covered their eyes.
Ⓑ They went near the windows.
Ⓒ They got down under their desks.
Ⓓ They moved the furniture.

24. What didn't the students do during the earthquake drill?

Ⓐ They didn't cover their heads.
Ⓑ They didn't hold on to their desks.
Ⓒ They didn't cover their eyes.
Ⓓ They didn't roll from side to side.

25. What did students in the hall do during the earthquake drill?

Ⓐ They went to their classrooms.
Ⓑ They went outside.
Ⓒ They sat down near an inside wall.
Ⓓ They rested on the floor.

26. Your clothing is on fire. What are you going to do?

Ⓐ Duck, cover, and hold.
Ⓑ Stop, drop, cover, and roll.
Ⓒ Cover my head with a desk or table.
Ⓓ Run to a window.

---

23 Ⓐ Ⓑ Ⓒ Ⓓ   24 Ⓐ Ⓑ Ⓒ Ⓓ   25 Ⓐ Ⓑ Ⓒ Ⓓ   26 Ⓐ Ⓑ Ⓒ Ⓓ

Go to the next page ⟩

G HOUSEHOLD REPAIR PROBLEMS

Choose the correct answer to complete the conversation.

Example:

My washing machine is broken.
You should call _____.

- Ⓐ a TV repairperson
- ● an appliance repairperson
- © an electrician
- Ⓓ a plumber

27. Somebody stole the keys to my apartment.
You should call _____.

- Ⓐ a carpenter
- Ⓑ a plumber
- © a painter
- Ⓓ a locksmith

28. Smoke comes into the room when we use the fireplace.
You should call _____.

- Ⓐ a chimneysweep
- Ⓑ the fire department
- © a carpenter
- Ⓓ a painter

29. Channels 2 through 50 are okay, but Channels 51 through 100 have a very bad picture.
We should call _____.

- Ⓐ an electrician
- Ⓑ an appliance repairperson
- © a TV repairperson
- Ⓓ the cable TV company

30. Look at all these bugs!
We should call _____.

- Ⓐ an electrician
- Ⓑ the animal control officer
- © an exterminator
- Ⓓ the zoo

31. I couldn't fix the doorbell.
Let's call _____.

- Ⓐ a locksmith
- Ⓑ an electrician
- © an appliance repairperson
- Ⓓ a mechanic

H GRAMMAR IN CONTEXT: Securing Household Repair Services

Choose the correct answer to complete the conversation.

Ex. There's _____ wrong with my bathroom sink. Can you send _____ to fix it?

- Ⓐ anything . . . anyone
- Ⓑ anyone . . . anything
- ● something . . . someone
- Ⓓ someone . . . something

33. I _____ be home at ten, but _____ be back at eleven.
Is 11:00 okay?

- Ⓐ won't . . . I'll
- Ⓑ won't . . . you'll
- © will . . . I'll
- Ⓓ will . . . you'll

32. I can't send _____ today. Will _____ be home tomorrow at 10 AM?

- Ⓐ somebody . . . somebody
- Ⓑ anybody . . . anything
- © anybody . . . somebody
- Ⓓ anything . . . something

34. Yes. _____ will be there at eleven.

- Ⓐ Anything
- Ⓑ Anybody
- © Something
- Ⓓ Someone

. . . .

27 Ⓐ Ⓑ © Ⓓ   29 Ⓐ Ⓑ © Ⓓ   31 Ⓐ Ⓑ © Ⓓ   33 Ⓐ Ⓑ © Ⓓ

28 Ⓐ Ⓑ © Ⓓ   30 Ⓐ Ⓑ © Ⓓ   32 Ⓐ Ⓑ © Ⓓ   34 Ⓐ Ⓑ © Ⓓ

Go to the next page ▷

I READING: First Aid Procedures

Choose the correct medical procedure for each emergency.

A	B	C	D
Cover the area with a cool wet cloth or put in cool water.	Try to remove stinger. Clean wound and apply cold cloth. Get medical help if there is itching, swelling, or if the person is dizzy, nauseous, or can't breathe.	Apply direct pressure with a clean cloth or sterile dressing directly on the wound.	If the victim cannot speak, breathe, or cough, ask for someone to call 911 and then perform the Heimlich maneuver.

Ex. bleeding
(A) (B) ● (D)

35. choking
(A) (B) (C) (D)

36. bee sting
(A) (B) (C) (D)

37. minor burn
(A) (B) (C) (D)

J LISTENING ASSESSMENT: An Emergency Call

Read and listen to the questions. Then listen to the conversation and answer the questions.

38. When did the person fall?
(A) While she was on a trip.
(B) While she was in her apartment.
(C) While she was on the phone.
(D) While she was walking down the stairs.

39. What's their address?
(A) 13 East Street.
(B) 13 West Street.
(C) 30 East Street.
(D) 30 West Street.

40. Where is their apartment?
(A) On the 5th floor.
(B) On the 6th floor.
(C) Apartment 6-C.
(D) Apartment 6-G.

K WRITING ASSESSMENT: Fill Out the Medical History Form

MEDICAL HISTORY

Name _____ Date of Birth ___ / ___ / ___
First   M. I.   Last   Month Day Year

Address _____ _____ _____ _____
Number Street   City   State   Zip Code

Telephone: Home _____ Work _____ Height _____ Weight _____

Emergency Contact: Name _____ Relationship _____ Telephone _____

Do you have:	YES	NO		YES	NO		YES	NO
heart disease?	☐	☐	allergies?	☐	☐	other problems?	☐	☐
kidney disease?	☐	☐	headaches?	☐	☐	Do you smoke?	☐	☐
high blood pressure?	☐	☐	trouble sleeping?	☐	☐	Do you drink?	☐	☐
diabetes?	☐	☐	trouble eating?	☐	☐	Are you taking medicine now?	☐	☐

If you answered Yes above, explain: _____

_____

L SPEAKING ASSESSMENT

I can ask and answer these questions:

Ask Answer
☐ ☐ How do you feel?
☐ ☐ When was your last appointment at a clinic or doctor's office?

Ask Answer
☐ ☐ Are you taking any medicine now?
☐ ☐ Is there any history of medical problems in your family? Explain.

Name _____

Date _____ Class _____

A **SCHOOL PERSONNEL & LOCATIONS**

Choose the correct answer.

Example:

The _____ is in the classroom.
Ⓐ custodian
● teacher
Ⓒ security officer
Ⓓ clerk

1. The _____ is in the library.
Ⓐ principal
Ⓑ security officer
Ⓒ librarian
Ⓓ science teacher

2. Our _____ is in the chemistry lab.
Ⓐ science teacher
Ⓑ English teacher
Ⓒ music teacher
Ⓓ school nurse

3. The _____ is in her office.
Ⓐ driver's ed instructor
Ⓑ librarian
Ⓒ security officer
Ⓓ principal

4. The _____ is in the cafeteria.
Ⓐ music teacher
Ⓑ custodian
Ⓒ clerk
Ⓓ security officer

5. The _____ is on the field.
Ⓐ principal
Ⓑ school nurse
Ⓒ P.E. teacher
Ⓓ science teacher

6. The _____ is in his office.
Ⓐ librarian
Ⓑ school nurse
Ⓒ clerk
Ⓓ guidance counselor

7. The _____ is in her classroom.
Ⓐ music teacher
Ⓑ English teacher
Ⓒ science teacher
Ⓓ P.E. teacher

8. The _____ is in the hall.
Ⓐ principal
Ⓑ driver's ed instructor
Ⓒ security officer
Ⓓ clerk

9. The _____ is in the parking lot.
Ⓐ P.E. teacher
Ⓑ driver's ed instructor
Ⓒ guidance counselor
Ⓓ security officer

10. The _____ is in the school office.
Ⓐ teacher
Ⓑ school nurse
Ⓒ security guard
Ⓓ clerk

11. Our _____ is in our classroom.
Ⓐ music teacher
Ⓑ English teacher
Ⓒ math teacher
Ⓓ science teacher

1 Ⓐ Ⓑ Ⓒ Ⓓ   4 Ⓐ Ⓑ Ⓒ Ⓓ   7 Ⓐ Ⓑ Ⓒ Ⓓ   10 Ⓐ Ⓑ Ⓒ Ⓓ
2 Ⓐ Ⓑ Ⓒ Ⓓ   5 Ⓐ Ⓑ Ⓒ Ⓓ   8 Ⓐ Ⓑ Ⓒ Ⓓ   11 Ⓐ Ⓑ Ⓒ Ⓓ
3 Ⓐ Ⓑ Ⓒ Ⓓ   6 Ⓐ Ⓑ Ⓒ Ⓓ   9 Ⓐ Ⓑ Ⓒ Ⓓ

B CLASSROOM INSTRUCTIONS

Choose the correct answer.

Example:

Open your _____.
- Ⓐ ruler
- Ⓑ pencil
- Ⓒ wall
- Ⓓ book   Ⓐ Ⓑ Ⓒ ●

12. Raise your _____.
- Ⓐ seat
- Ⓑ book
- Ⓒ hand
- Ⓓ computer

13. Erase the _____.
- Ⓐ board
- Ⓑ pencil
- Ⓒ pen
- Ⓓ globe

14. Take out a piece of _____.
- Ⓐ map
- Ⓑ dictionary
- Ⓒ book
- Ⓓ paper

15. Please hand in your _____.
- Ⓐ homework
- Ⓑ hand
- Ⓒ chair
- Ⓓ desk

16. Turn off the _____.
- Ⓐ map
- Ⓑ lights
- Ⓒ notebook
- Ⓓ ruler

C COMPUTER COMPONENTS

Look at the picture. Choose the correct word.

17.
- Ⓐ radio
- Ⓑ television
- Ⓒ monitor
- Ⓓ video

18.
- Ⓐ printer
- Ⓑ dictionary
- Ⓒ typewriter
- Ⓓ keyboard

19.
- Ⓐ notebook
- Ⓑ printer
- Ⓒ bookcase
- Ⓓ desk

20.
- Ⓐ mouse
- Ⓑ keyboard
- Ⓒ globe
- Ⓓ map

....

12 Ⓐ Ⓑ Ⓒ Ⓓ   **15** Ⓐ Ⓑ Ⓒ Ⓓ   **18** Ⓐ Ⓑ Ⓒ Ⓓ

13 Ⓐ Ⓑ Ⓒ Ⓓ   **16** Ⓐ Ⓑ Ⓒ Ⓓ   **19** Ⓐ Ⓑ Ⓒ Ⓓ

14 Ⓐ Ⓑ Ⓒ Ⓓ   **17** Ⓐ Ⓑ Ⓒ Ⓓ   **20** Ⓐ Ⓑ Ⓒ Ⓓ

Go to the next page ⟩

D GRAMMAR IN CONTEXT: School Registration

Choose the correct answer to complete the conversation.

21. I want to _____ for an English class.
- Ⓐ teach
- Ⓑ go
- Ⓒ register
- Ⓓ study

22. Okay. Please fill out this _____.
- Ⓐ want ad
- Ⓑ registration form
- Ⓒ job application form
- Ⓓ income tax form

23. With a pen or _____?
- Ⓐ a mouse
- Ⓑ a pencil
- Ⓒ a keyboard
- Ⓓ an eraser

24. A pen. And don't write. Please _____.
- Ⓐ print
- Ⓑ erase
- Ⓒ say
- Ⓓ type

E READING: A Class Schedule

Look at Gloria's class schedule. Choose the correct answer.

Time	Period	Class	Room
8:30-9:15	1st	P.E.	Gym
9:20-10:05	2nd	Math	217
10:10-10:50	3rd	English	115
10:55-11:40	4th	Social Studies	208
12:35-1:20	5th	Health	126
1:25-2:10	6th	Science	130
2:15-3:00	7th	Art	105

Example:

What does she study during fourth period?
- Ⓐ Health.
- Ⓑ Science.
- Ⓒ Social Studies.
- Ⓓ English.   Ⓐ Ⓑ ● Ⓓ

25. What does she study during second period?
- Ⓐ P.E.
- Ⓑ Health.
- Ⓒ Art.
- Ⓓ Math.

26. It's 2:00. What's she studying?
- Ⓐ Social Studies.
- Ⓑ English.
- Ⓒ Science.
- Ⓓ Health.

27. It's 10:30. Where is she?
- Ⓐ In Room 115.
- Ⓑ In the gym.
- Ⓒ In Room 130.
- Ⓓ In Room 105.

28. When does she study in Room 126?
- Ⓐ Third period.
- Ⓑ Fifth perod.
- Ⓒ Sixth period.
- Ⓓ Seventh period.

29. What time does her Science class begin?
- Ⓐ At 8:30.
- Ⓑ At 2:10.
- Ⓒ At 1:25.
- Ⓓ At 1:30.

30. What time does her 7th period class end?
- Ⓐ At 9:15.
- Ⓑ At 2:15.
- Ⓒ In Room 105.
- Ⓓ At 3:00.

....

21 Ⓐ Ⓑ Ⓒ Ⓓ   24 Ⓐ Ⓑ Ⓒ Ⓓ   27 Ⓐ Ⓑ Ⓒ Ⓓ   30 Ⓐ Ⓑ Ⓒ Ⓓ

22 Ⓐ Ⓑ Ⓒ Ⓓ   25 Ⓐ Ⓑ Ⓒ Ⓓ   28 Ⓐ Ⓑ Ⓒ Ⓓ

23 Ⓐ Ⓑ Ⓒ Ⓓ   26 Ⓐ Ⓑ Ⓒ Ⓓ   29 Ⓐ Ⓑ Ⓒ Ⓓ   Go to the next page ▷

F CLOZE READING: The Education System

There are many kinds of schools in the education system of the United States. Many young children go goes going to pre-school, but other children stayed stays stay ³¹ home or go to day-care centers. The one first last ³² year of public school for most children is kindergarten. In some school systems, children go from to with ³³ kindergarten for a full day. In other school systems, they we I ³⁴ go to school for half have heavy ³⁵ a day.

After kindergarten, children usually go to school for 12 days months years ³⁶. They go to elementary school, middle school, and high school. After that, many students

study studying studies ³⁷ in colleges, technical schools, and other institutions.

G LISTENING ASSESSMENT: Registration Procedures

Read and listen to the questions. Then listen to the conversation and answer the questions.

38. When DOESN'T the school have English classes?
   Ⓐ On Monday.
   Ⓑ On Friday.
   Ⓒ On Wednesday.
   Ⓓ On Saturday.

39. Where is Wendy going to write her personal information?
   Ⓐ On her driver's license.
   Ⓑ On a registration form.
   Ⓒ On a pen.
   Ⓓ On a short English test.

40. At what time AREN'T there any classes at this school?
   Ⓐ 10:00 A.M.
   Ⓑ 7:30 P.M.
   Ⓒ 2:00 P.M.
   Ⓓ 11:30 A.M.

H LEARNING SKILLS: Chronological Order & Steps in a Process

Put the classroom instructions in order.

_____ Write the answer.
_____ Sit down.
__1__ Stand up.
_____ Pick up the chalk.
_____ Go to the board.
_____ Put down the chalk.

Put the computer operations in order.

_____ Do your work.
_____ Insert the software disk.
_____ Eject the disk and turn off the computer.
_____ Open the software program.
_____ Save your work and close the program.
__1__ Turn on the computer.

I WRITING ASSESSMENT

Describe your school. Tell about the people, the classrooms, and other locations. (Use a separate sheet of paper.)

J SPEAKING ASSESSMENT

I can ask and answer these questions:
Ask Answer
☐ ☐ Where is our classroom?
☐ ☐ What's our class schedule?

31 Ⓐ Ⓑ Ⓒ Ⓓ   34 Ⓐ Ⓑ Ⓒ Ⓓ   37 Ⓐ Ⓑ Ⓒ Ⓓ   40 Ⓐ Ⓑ Ⓒ Ⓓ

32 Ⓐ Ⓑ Ⓒ Ⓓ   35 Ⓐ Ⓑ Ⓒ Ⓓ   38 Ⓐ Ⓑ Ⓒ Ⓓ

33 Ⓐ Ⓑ Ⓒ Ⓓ   36 Ⓐ Ⓑ Ⓒ Ⓓ   39 Ⓐ Ⓑ Ⓒ Ⓓ

STOP

A SMALL TALK AT WORK & AT SCHOOL

Choose the correct response.

Example:

What time is the break?
- Ⓐ It's on Friday.
- Ⓑ Every morning.
- ● It's at 10:30.
- Ⓓ Five days a week.

1. What's the weather forecast for tomorrow?
   - Ⓐ It's raining.
   - Ⓑ It's going to rain.
   - Ⓒ It rained.
   - Ⓓ It didn't rain.

2. I'm really tired today.
   - Ⓐ Congratulations!
   - Ⓑ That's great!
   - Ⓒ I'm glad to hear that.
   - Ⓓ I'm sorry to hear that.

3. It's very hot in the building today.
   - Ⓐ I agree. It's hot.
   - Ⓑ I agree. It isn't very hot.
   - Ⓒ I disagree. It's hot.
   - Ⓓ I disagree. It's very hot.

4. What kind of TV shows do you like?
   - Ⓐ You like news programs.
   - Ⓑ I like news programs.
   - Ⓒ I play baseball.
   - Ⓓ I like adventure movies.

5. Did you see the president on TV last night?
   - Ⓐ No, he wasn't.
   - Ⓑ No, you didn't.
   - Ⓒ Yes, I did.
   - Ⓓ Yes, you did.

6. Do you think Mr. Lawson will give a math test tomorrow?
   - Ⓐ I agree.
   - Ⓑ I disagree.
   - Ⓒ I think she will.
   - Ⓓ I think he will.

7. Do you think it'll rain tomorrow?
   - Ⓐ Maybe it will, and maybe it won't.
   - Ⓑ Maybe we will, and maybe we won't.
   - Ⓒ Maybe you will, and maybe you won't.
   - Ⓓ Maybe I will, and maybe I won't.

8. Do you think we'll have to work overtime?
   - Ⓐ Maybe we did, and maybe we didn't.
   - Ⓑ Maybe we do, and maybe we don't.
   - Ⓒ Maybe we will, and maybe we won't.
   - Ⓓ Maybe we are, and maybe we aren't.

9. Are you going out for lunch today?
   - Ⓐ No. I'm going to a restaurant.
   - Ⓑ No. I'm going to eat in my office.
   - Ⓒ Yes. I'm going to eat in my office.
   - Ⓓ Yes. I'm not going out for lunch.

1 Ⓐ Ⓑ Ⓒ Ⓓ   4 Ⓐ Ⓑ Ⓒ Ⓓ   7 Ⓐ Ⓑ Ⓒ Ⓓ

2 Ⓐ Ⓑ Ⓒ Ⓓ   5 Ⓐ Ⓑ Ⓒ Ⓓ   8 Ⓐ Ⓑ Ⓒ Ⓓ

3 Ⓐ Ⓑ Ⓒ Ⓓ   6 Ⓐ Ⓑ Ⓒ Ⓓ   9 Ⓐ Ⓑ Ⓒ Ⓓ

Go to the next page ⟩

B GRAMMAR IN CONTEXT: Invitations & Offers

Choose the correct answer to complete the conversations.

Example:

Would _____ like some milk?

Ⓐ you'll
⬤ you
Ⓒ you're
Ⓓ you do

10. _____ I'd love some.

Ⓐ Yes. Thanks.
Ⓑ No. Thanks.
Ⓒ No thank you.
Ⓓ Please don't.

11. Would you like to _____ with me after work today?

Ⓐ will have dinner
Ⓑ has dinner
Ⓒ having dinner
Ⓓ have dinner

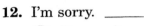

12. I'm sorry. _____

Ⓐ You can't.
Ⓑ You can.
Ⓒ I can't.
Ⓓ I can.

13. _____ you sure?

Ⓐ Do
Ⓑ Does
Ⓒ Is
Ⓓ Are

14. Yes. _____ work late.

Ⓐ I have to
Ⓑ I have
Ⓒ You have
Ⓓ I'm

15. _____ like to go sailing with me?

Ⓐ Did you
Ⓑ Did I
Ⓒ Would you
Ⓓ Would I

16. No, _____.

Ⓐ I don't
Ⓑ I don't think so
Ⓒ I think so
Ⓓ I think

17. Why _____?

Ⓐ don't
Ⓑ doesn't
Ⓒ no
Ⓓ not

18. _____ get seasick.

Ⓐ He might
Ⓑ I'm
Ⓒ I'm afraid I might
Ⓓ You're afraid

....

10 Ⓐ Ⓑ Ⓒ Ⓓ   13 Ⓐ Ⓑ Ⓒ Ⓓ   16 Ⓐ Ⓑ Ⓒ Ⓓ

11 Ⓐ Ⓑ Ⓒ Ⓓ   14 Ⓐ Ⓑ Ⓒ Ⓓ   17 Ⓐ Ⓑ Ⓒ Ⓓ

12 Ⓐ Ⓑ Ⓒ Ⓓ   15 Ⓐ Ⓑ Ⓒ Ⓓ   18 Ⓐ Ⓑ Ⓒ Ⓓ

Go to the next page ⟩

Name _____ **Date** _____

C GRAMMAR IN CONTEXT: Compliments

Choose the correct answer to complete the conversations.

Example:
_____ a very nice bicycle.
- (A) That
- ● That's
- (C) This
- (D) These

19. _____
- (A) It is that.
- (B) It's a bicycle.
- (C) Thanks.
- (D) You're welcome.

20. _____ fast?
- (A) Is it
- (B) It is
- (C) Are they
- (D) They are

21. Yes. It's _____ my old bicycle.
- (A) faster
- (B) faster than
- (C) more fast
- (D) more

22. These cookies _____ .
- (A) is delicious
- (B) more delicious
- (C) much more delicious
- (D) are delicious

23. Thanks. My new recipe is _____ my old one.
- (A) much better than
- (B) much better
- (C) more good
- (D) better

24. Your apartment _____ .
- (A) nicer than
- (B) is nicer than
- (C) is very nice
- (D) are very nice

25. Thank you. Do you like _____ ?
- (A) my sofa is new
- (B) my sofa is newer
- (C) my new sofa
- (D) newer sofa

26. Yes. It's _____ than your old one.
- (A) attractive
- (B) more attractive
- (C) much attractive
- (D) much more

27. I think so, too. It's also _____ comfortable.
- (A) much
- (B) good
- (C) better
- (D) more

19 (A) (B) (C) (D)   22 (A) (B) (C) (D)   25 (A) (B) (C) (D)

20 (A) (B) (C) (D)   23 (A) (B) (C) (D)   26 (A) (B) (C) (D)

21 (A) (B) (C) (D)   24 (A) (B) (C) (D)   27 (A) (B) (C) (D)

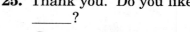

Go to the next page T45

Look at the TV listings. Choose the correct answer.

	6:00	6:30	7:00	7:30	8:00	8:30	9:00	9:30	10:00	10:30
2	News at 6 (News)	CBS Evening News (News)	Entertainment Tonight (Talk/Tabloid)	Who Wants to be a Millionaire (Game)	Life with Bobby: *Out to Lunch* (Comedy)	Everybody Loves Richard: *The Love Letter* (Comedy)	FBI Special Investigations Unit: *The Dangerous Package* (Crime)		PrimeTime Monday (Talk/Tabloid)	
4	Channel 4 News (News)	NBC Nightly News (News)	EXTRA (Talk/Tabloid)	Access Hollywood (Talk/Tabloid)	Happiest Class: *A New Teacher* (Comedy)	Wanda: *A Visitor from the Past* (Comedy)	Fletcher: *Bob's New Diet* (Comedy)	Fletcher: *Eat Your Vegetables* (Comedy)	Law & Order: *Bad Day at the Bank* (Crime)	
5	Everybody Loves Richard: *The First Day* (Comedy)	Everybody Loves Richard: *A New Friend* (Comedy)	Walt & Grace: *The Argument* (Comedy)	Neighbors: *The Lost Dog* (Comedy)	Biltmore Boys: *Alan's Problem* (Drama)		Three Sisters: *Trisha's New Boss* (Drama)		News at Ten (News)	
7	Eyewitness News (News)	ABC World News Tonight (News)	Jeopardy! (Game)	Wheel of Fortune (Game)	I'm With You: *Lost at the Mall* (Comedy)	Two by Two: *The School Dance* (Comedy)	According to Amy: *The Phone Message* (Comedy)	Better Than Ever: *Jim's New Couch* (Comedy)	LAPD Red: *Fight on the Freeway* (Crime)	
9	Baseball: *Anaheim Angels at Texas Rangers* (Sports) (Live)				KCAL 9 News at 8:00 PM		KCAL 9 News at 9:00 PM		KCAL 9 News at 10:00 PM (News)	Sports Central (News)
11	The Sampsons: *You're Fired!* (Cartoon)	Queen of the Hill: *Sally's New Car* (Comedy)	The Prince of Long Beach: *The Car Accident* (Comedy)	The Sampsons: *Henry's New Job* (Cartoon)	Downtown Medical Center: *Bad Day in the ER* (Reality)		Lost on an Island (Reality)		Fox 11 Ten O'Clock News (News)	
22	Cuanto Cuesta el Show (Game)		Noticias 22 (News)	El Tribunal del Pueblo (Reality)	El Hijo de Pedro Navajas (1986, Spanish)				Noticias 22 (News)	Contacto Deportivo (Sports/Info)
28	The NewsHour (News/Talk)		California's Golden Parks (Nature)	In the Kitchen (Cooking)	This Old Apartment: *Chicago* (Home Repair)		Great Performances: *Boston Symphony Orchestra in Moscow* (Concert)		NOVA: *Bugs, Bugs, Bugs* (Science)	

28. What's on Channel 5 at 7:00?
Ⓐ *EXTRA.*   Ⓒ *Jeopardy!*
Ⓑ *Walt & Grace.*   Ⓓ *Wheel of Fortune.*

29. What time is *Two by Two* on today?
Ⓐ 8:00.   Ⓒ Channel 2.
Ⓑ 8:30.   Ⓓ Channel 7.

30. What's on Channel 2 at 7:30?
Ⓐ A game show.   Ⓒ A news program.
Ⓑ A comedy show.   Ⓓ A cartoon program.

31. Which channel has programs in Spanish?
Ⓐ Channel 5.   Ⓒ Channel 22.
Ⓑ Channel 11.   Ⓓ Channel 28.

32. How many channels show the program *Everybody Loves Richard?*
Ⓐ One.   Ⓒ Three.
Ⓑ Two.   Ⓓ Four.

33. Which channels have news programs at 10:00?
Ⓐ 2, 4, 7.   Ⓒ 5, 9, 11.
Ⓑ 2, 4, 7, 28.   Ⓓ 5, 9, 11, 22.

34. My aunt loves classical music. What time is she going to watch TV today?
Ⓐ 7:00.   Ⓒ 9:00.
Ⓑ 8:00.   Ⓓ 10:00.

35. How many crime shows are on TV this evening?
Ⓐ One.   Ⓒ Three.
Ⓑ Two.   Ⓓ Four.

36. Which channel has the most news programs?
Ⓐ Channel 2.   Ⓒ Channel 7.
Ⓑ Channel 4.   Ⓓ Channel 9.

37. Which program isn't on tonight?
Ⓐ *Neighbors.*   Ⓒ *NOVA.*
Ⓑ *Friends.*   Ⓓ *LAPD Red.*

- -

28 Ⓐ Ⓑ Ⓒ Ⓓ   31 Ⓐ Ⓑ Ⓒ Ⓓ   34 Ⓐ Ⓑ Ⓒ Ⓓ   37 Ⓐ Ⓑ Ⓒ Ⓓ
29 Ⓐ Ⓑ Ⓒ Ⓓ   32 Ⓐ Ⓑ Ⓒ Ⓓ   35 Ⓐ Ⓑ Ⓒ Ⓓ
30 Ⓐ Ⓑ Ⓒ Ⓓ   33 Ⓐ Ⓑ Ⓒ Ⓓ   36 Ⓐ Ⓑ Ⓒ Ⓓ

Go to the next page ▷

E LISTENING ASSESSMENT: An Invitation

Read and listen to the questions. Then listen to the conversation and answer the questions.

38. What day is it?
- Ⓐ Tuesday.
- Ⓑ Wednesday.
- Ⓒ Thursday.
- Ⓓ We don't know.

39. What are they going to do tomorrow?
- Ⓐ Make dinner.
- Ⓑ Have dinner.
- Ⓒ Go to a class.
- Ⓓ Go to a meeting.

40. Where are they going to meet?
- Ⓐ At the restaurant.
- Ⓑ At the computer class.
- Ⓒ On Wednesday.
- Ⓓ At the person's office.

F CLOZE READING: Small Talk at Work

Circle the correct answers to complete the story.

"Small talk" of (at) when work is very important. Co-workers talk talks talking [1] with each other about many different things. They talk about my your their [2] favorite movies and TV programs. They talk above about with [3] music and sports. Much Many Co-workers [4] people also talk about the weather. Some subjects don't aren't isn't [5] very good for "small talk" in some countries, but in other countries this that these [6] subjects is are am [7] very common. For example, questions for about from [8] a person's salary or the price receipt how much [9] of a person's home are common in some countries are other but [10] very unusual in other countries.

G WRITING ASSESSMENT

Describe your plans for the weekend. What are you going to do? What might you do?

....

....

....

....

....

H SKILL ASSESSMENT: Making a Schedule

Fill out the chart with your schedule for a typical week. Write in your times at school, at work, at meetings, and at other events. Also write in the things you do to relax, including sports, favorite TV shows, and other evening and weekend activities

	MON	TUE	WED	THU	FRI	SAT	SUN
6:00 AM							
7:00							
8:00							
9:00							
10:00							
11:00							
12:00 Noon							
1:00 PM							
2:00							
3:00							
4:00							
5:00							
6:00							
7:00							
8:00							
9:00							
10:00							
11:00							

I SPEAKING ASSESSMENT

I can ask and answer these questions:

Ask Answer

☐ ☐ Tell about your typical schedule during the week.
☐ ☐ Tell about your typical schedule on the weekend.
☐ ☐ What TV programs do you usually watch? When?

T48

STOP

A SMALL TALK AT WORK & AT SCHOOL

Choose the correct response.

1. How do you like our new boss?
   I think she's _____ our old boss.
   - Ⓐ friendly
   - Ⓑ friendlier
   - Ⓒ friendlier than
   - Ⓓ more friendly

2. What do you think about our new English teacher?
   I think he's _____ our old teacher.
   - Ⓐ nicer
   - Ⓑ nicer than
   - Ⓒ more nice than
   - Ⓓ more nice

3. What's your favorite kind of music?
   Rock music. I think it's _____ other kinds of music.
   - Ⓐ better than
   - Ⓑ good than
   - Ⓒ more good than
   - Ⓓ more better than

4. The weather today is beautiful.
   I agree. It's _____ yesterday.
   - Ⓐ nice
   - Ⓑ nicer
   - Ⓒ nicer than
   - Ⓓ more nice than

5. I think your computer is newer than mine.
   It is. Mine is newer than _____.
   - Ⓐ my
   - Ⓑ mine
   - Ⓒ your
   - Ⓓ yours

6. Our math class isn't very interesting any more.
   I agree. It _____ more interesting.
   - Ⓐ to be used
   - Ⓑ used to be
   - Ⓒ used be to
   - Ⓓ was to be

7. Should I work overtime today or tomorrow?
   _____ work overtime today.
   - Ⓐ You think I should
   - Ⓑ You should I think
   - Ⓒ I think you should
   - Ⓓ I should you think

8. My locker isn't as clean as your locker.
   You're right. Mine _____ yours.
   - Ⓐ is cleaner than
   - Ⓑ isn't cleaner than
   - Ⓒ is as clean as
   - Ⓓ isn't as clean as

9. You know, the food in the cafeteria isn't as good as it used to be.
   I agree. The food _____.
   - Ⓐ is better now
   - Ⓑ are better now
   - Ⓒ used to be
   - Ⓓ used to be better

10. I think our science class is more interesting than our history class.
    I disagree. I think history _____ science.
    - Ⓐ isn't as interesting
    - Ⓑ isn't as interesting as
    - Ⓒ is more interesting
    - Ⓓ is more interesting than

1 Ⓐ Ⓑ Ⓒ Ⓓ   4 Ⓐ Ⓑ Ⓒ Ⓓ   7 Ⓐ Ⓑ Ⓒ Ⓓ   10 Ⓐ Ⓑ Ⓒ Ⓓ

2 Ⓐ Ⓑ Ⓒ Ⓓ   5 Ⓐ Ⓑ Ⓒ Ⓓ   8 Ⓐ Ⓑ Ⓒ Ⓓ

3 Ⓐ Ⓑ Ⓒ Ⓓ   6 Ⓐ Ⓑ Ⓒ Ⓓ   9 Ⓐ Ⓑ Ⓒ Ⓓ

Go to the next page ⟶

B GRAMMAR IN CONTEXT: Appropriate Language in Social Situations

Choose the correct answer to complete the conversations.

11. _____ You're stepping on my foot.
- (A) Excuse me.
- (B) Excuse.
- (C) You excuse me.
- (D) I excuse you.

12. Oh. _____
- (A) You apologize.
- (B) I apologize.
- (C) You're apologizing.
- (D) I'm apologizing.

13. That's okay. _____
- (A) Think.
- (B) Don't think.
- (C) Worry about it.
- (D) Don't worry about it.

14. _____
- (A) It's very sorry.
- (B) We're very sorry.
- (C) I'm really sorry.
- (D) You're really sorry.

15. You _____. Is something wrong?
- (A) are looking
- (B) look sad
- (C) sad
- (D) the matter

16. Yes. I have _____.
- (A) some bad news
- (B) some bad
- (C) some good news
- (D) some good

17. What _____?
- (A) happen
- (B) happened
- (C) happening
- (D) going to happen

18. My husband _____ yesterday.
- (A) lose job
- (B) lost job
- (C) lose his job
- (D) lost his job

19. I'm _____ that.
- (A) sorry
- (B) sorry to
- (C) sorry to hear
- (D) sorry hear

20. _____
- (A) Thank you.
- (B) I agree.
- (C) I disagree.
- (D) You're sorry.

11 (A)(B)(C)(D) 14 (A)(B)(C)(D) 17 (A)(B)(C)(D) 20 (A)(B)(C)(D)
12 (A)(B)(C)(D) 15 (A)(B)(C)(D) 18 (A)(B)(C)(D)
13 (A)(B)(C)(D) 16 (A)(B)(C)(D) 19 (A)(B)(C)(D)

C GRAMMAR IN CONTEXT: Asking for Clarification

Choose the correct answer to complete the conversations.

21. Will the train _____ soon?
- Ⓐ will arrive
- Ⓑ arrive
- Ⓒ going to arrive
- Ⓓ is going to arrive

22. Yes. _____ in five minutes.
- Ⓐ Arrive
- Ⓑ Going to arrive
- Ⓒ It arrive
- Ⓓ It'll arrive

23. _____
- Ⓐ In five minutes?
- Ⓑ It'll arrive?
- Ⓒ Yes, it will.
- Ⓓ No?

24. Yes. _____
- Ⓐ It's going to.
- Ⓑ You'll arrive.
- Ⓒ I will.
- Ⓓ That's right.

25. My birthday is _____ May 3rd.
- Ⓐ from
- Ⓑ with
- Ⓒ on
- Ⓓ at

26. May _____?
- Ⓐ who
- Ⓑ what
- Ⓒ why
- Ⓓ how

27. Where _____ you live?
- Ⓐ do
- Ⓑ does
- Ⓒ is
- Ⓓ are

28. I live _____ apartment 3-C.
- Ⓐ on
- Ⓑ with
- Ⓒ for
- Ⓓ in

29. _____ 3-G?
- Ⓐ Did you live
- Ⓑ Do you live
- Ⓒ Did you say
- Ⓓ Do you say

30. _____
- Ⓐ Yes. 3-G.
- Ⓑ Yes. 3-C.
- Ⓒ No. 3-G.
- Ⓓ No. 3-C.

. . . .

21 Ⓐ Ⓑ Ⓒ Ⓓ   24 Ⓐ Ⓑ Ⓒ Ⓓ   27 Ⓐ Ⓑ Ⓒ Ⓓ   30 Ⓐ Ⓑ Ⓒ Ⓓ

22 Ⓐ Ⓑ Ⓒ Ⓓ   25 Ⓐ Ⓑ Ⓒ Ⓓ   28 Ⓐ Ⓑ Ⓒ Ⓓ

23 Ⓐ Ⓑ Ⓒ Ⓓ   26 Ⓐ Ⓑ Ⓒ Ⓓ   29 Ⓐ Ⓑ Ⓒ Ⓓ

D CLOZE READING: A Thank-You Note

Choose the correct answers to complete the note.

Dear Alan,

Thank you [with (A) | for ● | by (C)] the wonderful dinner yesterday. [They (A) | It (B) | I (C)] ³¹ was

delicious. The vegetable soup [were (A) | was (B) | did (C)] ³² great, the hamburgers [were (A) | was (B) | are (C)] ³³

excellent, and the [potatoes (A) | carrots (B) | chili (C)] ³⁴ was also very good. In fact, I think your recipe

is much [good (A) | more good (B) | better (C)] ³⁵ than [my (A) | mine (B) | me (C)] ³⁶.

Thank you again. Next time [I'll (A) | I'm (B) | I (C)] ³⁷ invite you to MY place for dinner.

Sincerely,

Natalie

E LISTENING ASSESSMENT: Expressing Opinions

Read and listen to the questions. Then listen to the conversation and answer the questions.

38. What do they disagree about?
- (A) The buildings.
- (B) The streets.
- (C) The people.
- (D) The weather.

39. What do they agree about?
- (A) The people and the buildings.
- (B) The buildings and the parks.
- (C) The streets and the buildings.
- (D) The streets and the people.

40. Which opinion do they probably agree about?
- (A) The buildings in other cities are more interesting.
- (B) The people in other cities are friendlier.
- (C) The streets in other cities are cleaner.
- (D) The parks in other cities are more beautiful.

F WRITING ASSESSMENT

Compare two different places you know. Write about the streets, the buildings, the weather, the people, and life in these two places. (Use a separate sheet of paper.)

G SPEAKING ASSESSMENT

I can ask and answer these questions:

Ask Answer
- ☐ ☐ What's your favorite food?
- ☐ ☐ How do you like my new _____?
- ☐ ☐ What do you think about our English class?
- ☐ ☐ What's your opinion about life in our city?

- -

31 (A) (B) (C) (D)   34 (A) (B) (C) (D)   37 (A) (B) (C) (D)   40 (A) (B) (C) (D)

32 (A) (B) (C) (D)   35 (A) (B) (C) (D)   38 (A) (B) (C) (D)

33 (A) (B) (C) (D)   36 (A) (B) (C) (D)   39 (A) (B) (C) (D)

STOP

T52

APPENDIX

Listening Assessment Scripts

TEST 1a

Page T5, Section G

Read and listen to the questions.

38. What's his address?
39. When is his birthday?
40. How tall is he?

Now listen to the interview and answer the questions.

A. What's your name?
B. Victor Sanchez.
A. What's your address?
B. 94 Center Street in Reedville.
A. And your telephone number?
B. (978) 583–4712.
A. What's your date of birth?
B. May thirteenth, nineteen eighty-three.
A. And what's your height?
B. I'm five feet eight inches tall.

TEST 1b

Page T10, Section E

Read and listen to the questions.

37. Where is the 1-bedroom apartment?
38. How much is the rent on the 2-bedroom unit?
39. Which pets are allowed in the building?
40. How much is the security deposit on the 1-bedroom apartment?

Now listen to the conversation and answer the questions.

A. City Square Apartments. May I help you?
B. Yes. Do you have any apartments available?
A. Yes, we do. We currently have two apartments available. We have a one-bedroom unit on the fifth floor, and we have a two-bedroom unit on the sixth floor.
B. I see. And how much is the rent?
A. The apartment on the sixth floor is $1,100 per month. The one-bedroom rents for $800 per month.
B. Is there a security deposit?
A. Yes. A deposit of two months rent is required when you sign the lease.
B. Are pets allowed in the building?
A. Cats and smaller pets are allowed, but not dogs.
B. And is there an elevator in the building?
A. Yes. There are two. Would you like to make an appointment to see the units?
B. Yes, please.

TEST 2

Page T16, Section I

Read and listen to the questions.

37. When does the book club meet?
38. How many evening programs are there each month?
39. How many hours is the library open on Wednesdays?
40. On which date will the children's story hour meet?

Now listen to the library's recorded announcements and answer the questions.

This is the Central Library community events line. Here is the current listing of community events at the library. On the first Saturday of each month at 9 AM, children ages four to ten are invited to our children's story hour. On the third Thursday of each month, join librarian Kate Winters for the lunchtime book club. It meets in the community room at twelve noon. On the second and fourth Tuesdays of each month, come to our evening programs to learn about new books in the library collection. The programs start at 7:30. The Central Library is open Monday through Friday from 9 AM to 9 PM, Saturday from 9 AM to 6 PM, and Sunday from 1PM to 5 PM. Thank you for calling the Central Library community events line. Have a good day.

TEST 3

Page T20, Section H

Read and listen to the questions.

38. Where is the conversation taking place?
39. What is the customer going to have for an appetizer?
40. How many side orders is the customer going to have?

Now listen to the conversation and answer the questions.

A. Are you ready to order?
B. Yes, I am. I'd like the baked chicken, please.
A. All right. And what side order are you going to have with that?
B. Let me have an order of rice and an order of carrots, please.
A. Do you want a salad with your meal?
B. No, I don't think so.
A. And do you want to start with an appetizer this evening?
B. Let me see. Yes. Please give me a bowl of vegetable soup.
A. Anything to drink?
B. Yes. A glass of milk, please.

TEST 4

Page T24, Section F

Read and listen to the questions.

38. What does the person want to do?
39. What's the matter with the shoes?
40. Where is the conversation taking place?

Now listen to the conversation and answer the questions.

A. May I help you?
B. Yes, please. I want to return this dress and this pair of shoes.
A. What's the matter with them?
B. The dress is too long, and the shoes are too small.
A. I see. Do you want to exchange them?
B. No. I just want to return them, please.
A. All right. I'm afraid you can't return these items here in the Women's Clothing department. You can return them at the Customer Service counter.
B. Where is that?
A. It's upstairs on the third floor.
B. Thank you very much.

TEST 5

Page T32, Section H

Read and listen to the questions.

38. What kind of position is the person applying for?
39. Where is the conversation taking place?
40. How many years of work experience does the applicant have?

Now listen to the conversation and answer the questions.

A. Tell me about your skills.
B. I can type, and I can file.
A. Do you know how to use accounting software on a computer?
B. Yes. I used accounting software in my previous job.
A. Where was that?
B. I worked at the Johnson Insurance Company.
A. How long did you work there?
B. For three years.
A. And where did you work before that?
B. I worked at the Larsen Real Estate agency for two years, and before that I worked as a cashier at the Citywide Supermarket for one year.
A. And why are you interested in a position with us at Landmark Data Management?
B. I know this is an excellent company, and I think that I can be a very effective and useful employee here.

TEST 6

Page T38, Section J

Read and listen to the questions.

38. When did the person fall?
39. What's their address?
40. Where is their apartment?

Now listen to the conversation and answer the questions.

A. Emergency Operator.
B. I want to report an emergency.
A. Yes. Go ahead.
B. My mother tripped and fell while she was walking down the stairs in our building. She can't speak to me.
A. What's your address?
B. 30 East Street in Westville.
A. Is that an apartment building or a home?
B. An apartment building. We're on the sixth floor in Apartment 6-D.
A. Okay. Stay with your mother but don't move her. An ambulance is on the way.
B. Thank you.

TEST 7a

Page T42, Section G

Read and listen to the questions.

38. When DOESN'T the school have English classes?
39. Where is Wendy going to write her personal information?
40. At what time AREN'T there any classes at this school?

Now listen to the conversation and answer the questions.

A. May I help you?
B. Yes. My name is Wendy Chen. I want to study English. Do you have English classes at this school?
A. Yes, we do. We have classes five days a week, Monday through Friday, in the morning and in the evening. Here's a registration form. Please print all your personal information in ink. Do you have a pen?
B. Yes, I do.
A. And do you have a document with your address?
B. Yes. I have a driver's license.
A. Good. Complete the form. Then give me the form and show me your driver's license. Then you're going to take a short English test.
B. Okay. Thank you.

TEST 7b

Page T47, Section E

Read and listen to the questions.

38. What day is it?
39. What are they going to do tomorrow?
40. Where are they going to meet?

Now listen to the conversation and answer the questions.

A. Would you like to have dinner with me after work today?
B. I'm sorry. I can't. I go to a computer class every Tuesday after work.
A. How about tomorrow? Would you like to have dinner tomorrow?
B. Tomorrow? Yes. I'd love to.
A. Great. I'll meet you at five at your office. Okay?
B. Great.

TEST 8

Page T52, Section E

Read and listen to the questions.

38. What do they disagree about?
39. What do they agree about?
40. Which opinion do they probably agree about?

Now listen to the conversation and answer the questions.

A. You know, I think the streets in our city aren't as clean as they used to be.
B. I think so, too. But I think the buildings in our city are very interesting.
A. Do you really think so? In my opinion, the buildings in other cities around here are MORE interesting.
B. What do you think about the people in our city?
A. I think they're very friendly. Do you agree?
B. Definitely. And I think our parks are very beautiful.
A. I don't think so.